REFLECTIVE LEARNING FOR SOCIAL WORK

For Hilary, Miles and Alice; Roger, Ben and Nicholas.

Reflective Learning
for
Social Work

Research, Theory and Practice

Edited by
Nick Gould and Imogen Taylor

arena

Published by
Arena
Ashgate Publishing Limited
Gower House
Croft Road
Aldershot
Hants GU11 3HR
England

Ashgate Publishing Company
Old Post Road
Brookfield
Vermont 05036
USA

British Library Cataloguing in Publication Data

Reflective learning for social work:
  research, theory and practice
  1. Social work education
  2. Social service
  I. Gould, Nick   II.   Taylor, Imogen
  361.3'07

Library of Congress Catalog Card Number: 96-84530

ISBN 1 85742 321 6 (paperback)
ISBN 1 85742 320 8 (hardback)

Typeset in Palatino by Raven Typesetters, Chester and printed in Great Britain by Hartnolls Ltd, Bodmin

Contents

List of contributors

Jane Batchelor is Lecturer in Social Work at the University of Bath, UK.

David Boud is Professor of Adult Education in the School of Adult Education at the University of Technology, Sydney, Australia.

Karen Boutland is Joint Co-ordinator of the Practice Learning Centre at the University of Bath, UK.

Brian Dimmock is Lecturer in Health and Social Welfare at the Open University, UK.

Nick Gould is Senior Lecturer and head of research and consultancy at the Social Services Research and Development Unit, University of Bath, UK.

Susan Knights is Senior Lecturer and co-ordinator of the BEd in Adult Education in the School of Adult Education at the University of Technology, Sydney, Australia.

Ken Moffatt is Assistant Professor at King's College, University of Western Ontario, London, Canada.

Catherine P. Papell is Professor Emeritus at the School of Social Work, Adelphi University, New York, USA.

Phyllida Parsloe is Professor of Social Work at the University of Bristol, UK.

Amy B. Rossiter teaches in the School of Social Work at York University, Toronto, Canada.

Imogen Taylor is Lecturer in Social Work at the University of Bristol, UK.

Acknowledgements

Above all, we acknowledge the crucial role of our contributors whose work both inspires and extends the debate about reflective learning. Our thanks also to colleagues at the Universities of Bristol and Bath whose support and stimulation have helped this book come to fruition. Equally significant have been the students who over the years have contributed to our own reflective learning. Finally, we are deeply grateful to Jo Campling for her encouragement at an early stage of the project and Alison Brady for producing the manuscript.

1 Introduction: social work education and the 'crisis of the professions'

Nick Gould

What kinds of knowledge do skilled social work practitioners bring to bear on their practice? What are the components of this knowledge – is it cognitive, behavioural, attitudinal, affective or multidimensional? How is this knowledge acquired, maintained and developed? Such questions inevitably become the pre-occupation of social work educators, whether they are academics located in institutions of higher education, or trainers based in practice agencies with a responsibility for student practice learning or staff development. This volume presents an international collection of writing by authors whose interest in such questions – whether arising from educational research, teaching social work, or practice as specialists in adult education – has led them to engagement with the concept of reflective learning.

The reflective learning paradigm starts from an attempt to understand how social workers make judgements and decisions in domains which are uncertain and complex. There is considerable empirical evidence, based on research into a variety of occupations, suggesting that expertise does not derive from the application of rules or procedures applied deductively from positivist research. Instead, it is argued that practice wisdom rests upon highly developed intuition which may be difficult to articulate but can be demonstrated through practice. On the basis of this reconstructed epistemology of practice, reflective learning offers an approach to education which operates through an understanding of professional knowledge as primarily developed through practice and the systematic analysis of experience. This is sometimes referred to as a theory of experiential learning, although this is a term open to misunderstanding in social work, being often trivialized as a general reference to techniques such as role play and simulation exercises. Although already influential in other areas of professional education, reflective learning as a distinct educational theory has so far only been tentatively examined in the social work literature but is indicated by reference to such concepts as 'reflective learning', 'reflective practice', 'reflection-in-action' and 'the reflective learning environment'.

There is always a danger that a concept such as reflective learning will become little more than a slogan. The contributors to this volume offer a range of definitions of what they mean by reflection, but the commonality is that they are all engaging at some level with the application in social work of the ideas of Donald Schön, but often refracted through other influences. For instance, there is the work of John Dewey, who identified the centrality of reflection as a process through which learning from experience takes place (Dewey 1933). Experience, Dewey argued, is the organizing focus for learning; observations and actions are synthesized with conceptual ideas leading to higher-order practice. Kolb has more recently been highly influential in formalizing these ideas into a cyclical model of experiential learning, a feedback loop by which experience is acted upon through reflective observation, leading to abstract conceptualization, on the basis of which active experimentation produces modified practice intervention (Kolb 1984). Critical theory has also provided inspiration for approaches to reflective learning; in particular, Carr and Kemmis, influenced by Habermas's conception of communicative action, have extended the idea of the practitioner as an action-researcher who is constantly testing and critiquing theories of action through situated practice (Carr and Kemmis 1986).

However, above all the concept of reflective learning has become associated with the work of Donald Schön, through his seminal works, *The Reflective Practitioner* (1983) and *Educating the Reflective Practitioner* (1987). Schön's work is based upon qualitative, idiographic case studies of practitioners in the fields of engineering, town planning, architecture, management and clinical psychology, but his ideas have been applied in many other areas of professional education, in particular teacher education. Schön's work begins from a critique of those classical models of technical rationality which suggest that positivist knowledge can be applied to real-life problems in a deductive and direct way. Schön has inverted this conventional understanding of the relationship between theory and practice (the simplistic idea that theory is applied deductively to practice), demonstrating that significant dimensions of 'theory' are only revealed through skilled practice, are implicit in action and often beyond conscious articulation. Similarly, professional 'problems' are not ontologically pre-defined, but have to be constructed through engagement by the practitioner with the 'indeterminate zone of practice' which is typically characterized by uncertainty, uniqueness and value conflict (Schön 1987, p. 6). A not uncommon illustration of this might be a duty social worker, called to the police station to assess someone arrested for a breach of the peace because the arresting officer thinks the person may be suffering from a mental disorder. Whether the professional social work issues raised by this situation relate primarily to criminality, a mental health crisis or some other problem still to be discovered such as homelessness, is not pre-determined at the point of referral, but is negotiated via a complex series of transactions between the worker, the detained individual and possibly other actors such as police or psychiatrists.

From this perspective, positivist knowledge and formal theory are not neutral resources which can be drawn down and directly applied, but are only of use when mediated through the complex filters of practice experience. In order to become a tool for practice, the practitioner has to transform theory in the light of learning from past experience (reflection-on-action), and through improvisation during the course of intervention (reflection-in-action). As Michael Eraut has commented, practitioners are directly engaged in the processes of knowledge creation, there is not a one-way transmission of knowledge from academia to practice. This requires academics responsible for professional studies to re-direct at least some of their skills so that they are, 'enhancing the knowledge creation capacities of individuals and professional communities' (Eraut 1985, p. 117).

Social work and the crisis of social work education

Schön placed his own work within a discussion of an apparent 'crisis of the professions', produced by growing public scepticism as to the infallibility of practitioners, a reduction in automatic deference to professionals, and the inevitable extension of this mood to the belief that the education and preparation of new professionals has become inadequate. Some might think that social work has had more than a fair share of its own crises. Commentators have sought to locate the malaise of social work education within various explanatory frameworks. One argument is that the difficulties lie in the particular nature of social work practice, that it typically requires practitioners to integrate the instrumental and the expressive, the affective and the cognitive. This habitually brings academic social work departments into conflict with their host institutions where universities have traditionally supported a status hierarchy of knowledge. Experimental research is the exemplar of 'real' academic work, and applied knowledge is accorded an inferior position and only tolerated insofar as it can demonstrate a technical-rational approach to the application of scientific knowledge in practical settings. The impact of this form of institutionalized epistemological discrimination is often manifested in the insecurity of academic social work departments and difficulties of individual staff attaining tenure.

Studies of reflective practice bear out many of the lessons of recent research in the sociology of scientific knowledge (e.g. Collins 1992, 2nd edn), showing that in fact the supposedly rigorous scientific disciplines such as medicine or laboratory research are just as contingent upon the mediation of practice skills, human judgement, intuition, artistry and tacit knowledge as the supposedly 'fuzzy' vocations such as teaching and social work. Schön's analysis of skilled practice in a range of disciplines is also a meta-theory of practice which shows the commonalities between disciplines which have traditionally occupied different points in the academic status hierarchy. The reflective model collapses the cognitive-affective dichotomy by showing that practice knowledge is organized around experientially-based schema which transcend oppositions of feeling and fact.

The reflective learning debates also incorporate the ongoing controversies about the relationship between theory and practice which dispute the content of the academic disciplinary knowledge base for social work; for instance, is it a form of applied social science to which any combination of psychology, sociology or social policy make a foundational contribution, or should the humanities, e.g. literary criticism, provide a more appropriate knowledge base for social work (England 1986)? Or, from the reflective perspective, should theories be seen as providing alternative frames or metaphors which are more or less helpful positions from which practice can be reviewed and deconstructed, but without any one discipline constituting a bedrock of knowledge which can be said to be foundational?

A further critique within the crisis of social work education has been the functionalist argument that the problems of social work education are a product of organizational expansion and transformations of social work bureaucracies. This argument is advanced on two fronts: first, that the profession has broadened its definition of social work to become a highly diversified activity; and secondly, social work organizations have increased dramatically in size, incorporating a wider range of social service activities than were within earlier definitions of social work. The newly-qualified social worker is expected to operate competently not only in a variety of settings with a multiplicity of client groups, but also at various levels of the organization.

Within British social work these tensions seem to have produced at least two effects. The first is the concerted attempt by employers to gain control over qualifying social work education, in the belief that the employer knows what social workers really need to know and do. The second (and related) effect has been the ascendancy of the competency-based approach to learning which suggests that complex activities such as social work intervention can be digitized into discrete actions or competencies, which are measurable outcomes of any training programme. Although its genealogy has become glossed over and submerged, the origins of competency-based approaches to education lie both in positivist behaviourism and also new managerialist demands for accountability in public services (Richardson 1990). The effect, at least in British social work education in the 1990s, has been pressure to accept a severe intellectual reductionism which treats everything from professional ethics to legal knowledge as 'competencies' to be ticked off from a functionalist checklist. The consequences of these trends are a downgrading of critical analysis as an educational objective and a short-term view of practice to suit the supposed labour force requirements of agencies. A recent review of the quality of social work education in English universities concluded that, 'this focus [upon competence] may sometimes limit the provision of a broader and broadening professional education, which takes a longer-term view of personal and professional development' (Higher Education Funding Council for England 1995, p. 10). In contrast to this, reflective learning recognizes that a purpose of education is to facilitate people as (in Bateson's terms) double-loop learners who are able to challenge the normative context of practice, and to be non-defensive and adaptive learners within a constantly evolving professional environment (Bateson 1973).

All this is not to suggest that Schön's model of reflective learning is a finished project, written in tablets of stone. If reflective learning is to be a dynamic influence then the theory has to be seen as reflexive, being itself transformed by the processes of educators using the ideas and learning through that experience. This collection of writings is part of that process, as social work and adult educators describe and evaluate their own experience. Indeed, social work's continuous preoccupation with the configuration of the person in the social environment makes it a particularly interesting site for the exploration of organizational, social and political implications of reflective learning. Schön's work is process orientated and methodologically individualistic, but many of the following chapters shows the apparent paradox that the creation of personal knowledge is a very social process. This inevitably brings into the conceptual frame issues of power relationships, both in the professional setting and the classroom. A potent aspect of those power relationships is gender, and these studies frequently draw upon feminist theories as centrally important in understanding not only these connections between personal and public knowledge, but also in legitimizing research methodologies which are sensitive and alert to the challenges of empowerment and emancipation. Similarly, professional education invariably occurs within an organizational context, be it the agency or classroom; the challenges and opportunities which exist as a consequence of organizational structure, management approaches, culture and not least of all the design of the curriculum, are all constitutive of the concerns of reflective learning.

The themes introduced in this chapter become amplified and extended by Catherine Papell in Chapter 2 where she considers implications of reflective learning for contemporary social work education. Although these are instanced within a North American context, the issues raised are internationally relevant. The reflective paradigm carries implications for social work education in relation to three issues discussed by Papell. First, it confirms the centrality of experiential learning within the formation of practice knowledge. Intellectually, this recognition receives validity from challenges to the dominance of positivism which come from research methodologies which are qualitative and heuristic. Secondly, reflective learning brings to attention the relationship between generalist perspectives and specialism, and the academic levels at which these are appropriately developed. Thirdly, it reconstructs understanding of the relationship between theoretical knowledge and the nature of social reality. All these issues influence not only processes of learning and teaching, but also the way curricula are created, and the relationship of professional education to the wider system of higher education.

This last theme is taken up in David Boud and Susan Knights' chapter on course design for reflective practice. Writing from their experiences as university-based adult educators in Australia, they argue that the encouragement of reflective practice requires more than the piecemeal adding on of ways of debriefing periods of field work; it requires deeper level integration of appropriate ways to build notions of reflective practice into the processes of teaching and learning through programmes. Reflection should not be seen as something which is separate from the normal teaching and learning practices of a course; Boud and Knights outline a range of strategies for incorporating reflective practice into activities which serve other teaching values and content objectives. These approaches support a three-stage model of learning from experience which involves learners in returning to the experience, attending to feelings connected with the experience and revaluating the experience. As part of this process the learning milieu is given particular prominence, within which the curriculum and the teacher figure strongly.

A concluding thought from Boud and Knights is that if reflection is not to be just an uncritically received 'hurrah' concept then good research evidence is needed to help understand the processes acting upon reflective learning. In Chapter 4 Alma Harris reports findings from a two-year longitudinal study into experiential learning in social work. Types of experience which proved significant to students choosing social work as a career are explored, along with the experience of students during their placement and their effect on professional development. In particular Harris concentrates on the ways in which students conceptualize their learning from experience. She finds that initially students have very technicist views of how their past life experience provides opportunities for rehearsal and practice of professional skills. The experience of supervised practice in fieldwork placements led to students developing more extended repertoires of 'knowing-in-action', but the process by which this occurs is highly dependent on the cues and opportunities for reflection provided by a mentor. The outcome of such exploration is likely to be a more complex but coherent model of practice.

Boud and Knights also draw attention in Chapter 3 to the importance of integrating strategies for promoting reflection within teaching programmes, and Chapters 5, 6 and 7 provide illumination of contrasting aspects of this task. There are few examples within the social work education literature of description and analysis of the actual classroom teaching process. As a corrective to this Ken Moffatt offers from Canada both a conceptual framework and description of his experience of teaching social work practice as a reflective process to final year undergraduates. He locates his approach to teaching within a theoretical synthesis which draws together feminist writing on caring, social work literature on interpretive methods, and Bourdieu's work on the concept of social fields, in order to characterize the position of social work practitioners within bureaucratic welfare institutions. Moffatt then shows how these sources were drawn upon in working with students in a three-stage programme of lecture and discussion, reflection on practice through role play and journal writing, and further lecture and discussion. His experience shows how students develop complexity in their analysis of their own practice, bringing forward judgements which had seemingly been based on unproblematic 'common-sense' for rigorous analysis and deconstruction. The author shows how the reflective approach can provide a sophisticated form of critique which overcomes the static and reductionist oppositions of micro- and macro-level interventions, or subjective and objective factors.

The limitations of categorical and dichotomous thought is a central concern of important recent debates within social theory, drawing upon various sources such as social constructivism, discourse theory and post-Wittgensteinian analytic philosophy. One of the topics which emerges from these studies is an interest in how imagery and metaphor operate as schema through which the individual organizes his or her knowledge of the world and acts within it. Imagery is socially and experientially produced and thereby also provides an important source for understanding how professional identity is constructed. Brought within the learning situation the exploration of imagery provides a powerful medium for students to examine values, attitudes and behaviour in an integrated way. In Chapter 6, Nick Gould describes action research, repertory grid technique and the use of art as approaches within social work education which can make a powerful contribution to reflection on action.

All of these techniques and methods have radical implications for the conventional role of the social work teacher, limiting the traditional place of didactic pedagogy, and supplementing it with tasks and approaches which often resonate with social group work. This is particularly relevant to the development of self-directed and problem-led learning. In Chapter 7, Imogen Taylor reviews the requirements upon social work educators to act as facilitators to these processes of self-direction. This includes providing structures through which reflective learning can be supported, such as the design of 'problems' for students to work on, learning activities and resources and the enabling qualities needing to be demonstrated by the facilitator. All this is illustrated through the author's experiences of the development of Enquiry and Action Learning at the University of Bristol.

The emphasis so far has been on the practice of social work education in the classroom. It has been a long-established feature of social work education that learning in the academic institution must be complemented by supervised practice in direct-service agencies. This brings into focus the characteristics of the organization as a learning environment, and the skills of the mentor (in the British social work context known as the practice teacher) in enhancing reflective learning as an active process, rather than the student being a passive object of socialization. In Chapter 8, Jane Batchelor and Karen Boutland describe a piece of action research at the University of Bath's practice learning centre to develop and evaluate a model of practice learning called the network placement. This provides opportunity for students to work within more than one agency during a single placement, under the supervision of an external supervisor to manage the logistics of such a complex arrangement, and to help students make a coherent experience out of contrasting settings. The authors show how the network placement not only broadens the experience of the student, but the essentially comparative nature of the placement can powerfully enhance reflective learning, by highlighting through different aspects of agency organization and policy, the practitioner role and intervention skills. Implications for practice teachers in managing network placements are considered, in particular the need to negotiate clear lines of accountability and responsibility for assessment, if the benefits are to be maximized.

Chapters 9 and 10 are concerned with management for reflective practice, but provide contrasts between, on the one hand, management within agencies of practitioner teams, while the other provides a rare insider view of the practice of managing an academic social work department within a university. In Chapter 9 Phyllida Parsloe analyses the experience of having been professor of social work and head of department in two British universities. As has been discussed earlier in this chapter, Schön's work very much began from a consideration of the relationship between epistemology and status in academic institutions; this chapter provides a reflective analysis of the experience of mediating between a discipline (social work) which traditionally has problems of legitimacy and status within hierarchical and patriarchal university cultures, whilst at the same time introducing a pedagogic approach which exemplifies the self-directed, experiential modes which are inimical to those cultures.

Brian Dimmock provides the contrast of using consultancy to promote reflective practice amongst social workers within an agency in which social work is by definition the host and dominant culture. Here the primary task is to cultivate the habits of reflection in a milieu where the resources of time and psychological space are limited, but the pressures arising from organizational change and the external demand for services are great. Drawing on strategies used in systemic family therapy, practitioners are encouraged to construct narratives which illuminate dilemmas, and to find more productive analytical 'frames' for encouraging attitudinal and behavioural change. These examples are drawn upon to illuminate the contrast between expert and reflective approaches to management consultancy.

It has been mentioned that if reflective learning is to be an authentic and radical theory of experiential learning for social work then it should also be reflexive, challenging the ideological neutrality of conventional academic discourse, and validating the authenticity of the educator's experience. Amy B. Rossiter begins from an examination of the impact upon herself of watching a play in the theatre depicting alienation and disempowerment, and connects this to her own feelings about the social work theory which provides the content of much social work teaching but which conceals many of the aspects of domination and inequality which social work is supposed to challenge. Postmodernism, combined with studies of gender, race and class, make the relationships between knowledge and power visible not only as aspects of a reality 'out there' but also as characteristics of relationships within the teaching situation. Rossiter considers the opportunities which have to be created within social work education for students to connect their own experience of social reality to academic discourses, and for the educator to risk the challenges to control and mastery which this process can create.

Finally, in Chapter 12 Imogen Taylor considers key issues which have emerged throughout the book, highlighting recurring themes, and discussing their relevance for social work education but within the context of professional education generally. Future prospects for reflective learning are also examined in the context of present trends in higher education towards more students and fewer resources, and trends in practice towards emphases on outcomes and competence.

References

Bateson, G. (1973), *Steps to an Ecology of Mind: Collected Essays in Anthropology, Psychiatry, Evolution and Epistemology*. St. Albans: Paladin.

Carr, W. and Kemmis, S. (1986), *Becoming Critical*. Lewes: Falmer Press.

Collins, H. (1992, 2nd edn), *Changing Order: Replication and Induction in Scientific Practice*. Chicago: University of Chicago Press.

Dewey, J. (1933), *How We Think*. Boston: D.C. Heath & Co.

England, H. (1986), *Social Work As Art*. London: Allen and Unwin.

Erault, M. (1985), 'Knowledge Creation and Knowledge Use in Professional Contexts', *Studies in Higher Education*, **10** (1), 117–37.

Higher Education Funding Council for England (1995), *Quality Assessment of Applied Social Work*. Bristol: HEFCE.

Kolb, D.A. (1984), *Experiential Learning: Experience as the Source of Learning and Development*. Englewood Cliffs, NJ: Prentice Hall.

Richardson, V. (1990), 'The evolution of reflective teaching and teacher education', in R. Clift, W.R. Houston and M. Pugach (eds), *Encouraging Reflective Practice in Education: An Analysis of Issues and Programs*. New York: Teachers College Press.

Schön, D.A. (1983), *The Reflective Practitioner*. London: Temple Smith.

Schön, D.A. (1987), *Educating the Reflective Practitioner: Towards a New Design for Teaching and Learning in the Professions*. San Francisco: Jossey Bass.

2 Reflections on issues in social work education[1]

Catherine P. Papell

Three dialectical issues for social work education, in the 1990s and the turn of the century, have bearing on the concept of learning for reflective practice. These are (i) the issue between academic education and experiential learning, (ii) the issue between a generalist perspective and specialization, and (iii) the issue between theoretical knowledge and the nature of the real social world. I call these issues dialectical because there are powerful opinions and opposing positions involved – in the first instance, from outside the profession, in the second instance, from within the profession, and in the third, both from within and without the profession of social work. A discussion of these issues may challenge the thinking of the learner, the teacher and the curriculum planner, and may foster a reflective quality in the social worker's understanding of his/her profession and practice.

These issues, while marked in North American social work education, are undoubtedly played out wherever the social work profession is striving and straining to emerge and thrive on behalf of human well-being.

Academic education and experiential learning

Early on in the history of North American social work, the decision was deliberately made that education for professional practice would be seated in the university. Experiential learning with academic credit would be a basic component of the education and it would be provided by the agencies in a collaborative arrangement between school and field. However, the practicum component of professional social work education and academe's technical–rational paradigm for developing and transmitting knowledge (Schön 1983, 1987) have not existed together without tension.

From the strain of the uneasy relationship between university and agency

11

there have emerged many creative patterns for educating through field practice, e.g. training for agency field instructors (supervisors) by the schools of social work, attempts to develop 'curriculum' for field practice, academic curricular designs combining practice class and field, university-based service centres with field instruction carried out by academic faculty, agency staff invited to teach as adjuncts in the academic practice courses, and block placements. Any of these, and other designs, are variations on the theme of academically credited, concurrent experiential learning as an inviolate aspect of social work education. The importance of field work to the learner has been confirmed again and again in studies carried out in schools of social work in North America.

The technical–rational paradigm has been described (Schön 1983) as deficient and incompatible with education for any of the professions because it assumes that the ends or outcomes of professional problem solving can be known and determined in advance of the process. The paradigm also assumes that the builder of knowledge can be truly neutral, not influenced by his/her own sensations, social contexts or knowledge systems. One impact of academe's positivist, technical–rationalism on social work's educational traditions and tasks is exemplified in the efforts to develop quantitative research as the scientific component in its knowledge base.[2]

An alternative paradigm, set forth by Schön, for educating any professional, since action or doing is required is 'reflection-in-action'. The relevance of the paradigm of the reflective practitioner to social work education was summarized in its essential elements (Papell and Skolnik 1992, p. 20). These were found to be:

I   the acknowledgement of a need for a specific epistemology of practice;
II   the rejection of linear thinking as the primary mode for professional problem solving and knowledge building;
III the recognition that every professional encounter is unique, and cannot be fully explicated by immanent theory;
IV   the elevation of art, intuition, creativity and practice wisdom to essential places in professional functioning;
V   the perception of the potential for knowledge-building through the research processes inherent in reflective practice.

Citing Virginia Robinson, Charlotte Towle and Bertha Reynolds, it was shown (pp. 20–21) how social work educators and theory builders, throughout our North American history, have written within the framework of these very elements.

There are also strong contemporary trends within the social work profession that stand confidently in opposition to the pressures of the technical–rational and positivist traditions. This is evidenced by the growing interest in qualitative research which might be metaphorically described as a movement in the field (Sherman and Reid 1994).

Inherent in qualitative research, whether acknowledged or not, is the 'heuristic paradigm' (Tyson 1992). This paradigm takes issue with the tendency that has prevailed in the profession to elevate the positivist paradigm as the only satisfactory source for the building of social work knowledge and producing 'truth' and justification for our practice. The heuristic paradigm insists that no knowledge can be neutral since it is always constructed through the lenses of the researcher, whose choices in the perception of the problem and in the questions asked affect the knowledge that is produced. Tyson states that though neutrality is impossible, bias can be regulated by recognition, and the value of the finding can be seen in the context of the heuristic, or point of view, used by the practitioner-researcher (p. 550).[3] The field work setting, wherein the perception of the social situation is required in order to use knowledge, and the university, wherein the formal building of knowledge takes place, can thus be linked by recognition of congruent reflective processes.

Some additional contemporary challenges to the positivist, technical–rational paradigm by North American social work educators, theoreticians and practitioners are found in the social constructionist approach.[4] The linkage between experiential learning for practice skill and theoretical and conceptual learning in the university classroom is exemplified and/or strengthened by the authors or teams of authors who write on this approach. Such writings are representative of the contributions that social workers are making toward an epistemology of practice.

A recent publication from educational psychology (Moustakas 1990) sets forth a similar concern in the related professional field. The author's rigour and creativity can suggest for social work students – and their teachers – how knowledge about the human condition can be found by listening directly and systematically to those who are experiencing it. The search for knowledge starts from *within* both the subject *and* the researcher (p. 15) rather than with deductive abstractions in which variables that cannot be controlled have been eliminated. Meaning is to be found by pursuing the complexities of the subject (pp. 38–9). Moustakas' study of loneliness is presented along with other examples of the methodology. The author's clinical point of view and commitment to knowing more and more about the experience of being human is a celebration of disciplined subjectivity.

In the experiential learning that takes place in the social work field practicum, a fundamental task is teaching the learner how to use knowledge, how theory can be helpful in illuminating the practice situation. But it is also a fundamental task to help the student to tune in to his/her own subjectivity (in social work we have usually called it 'self-awareness'), to trust feelings and contain them in the interest of the responsibility of the professional role.

Understanding the concept of countertransference is crucial in helping processes. However, more than learning the concept, the goal for the social work student is knowing and appreciating the emotional world of self and others.

Through field practice, the student can learn to allow life and experience as well as formal knowledge to influence and enrich the growing professional self. If a helping goal for our clients is to enable them to recognize their feeling worlds and to find 'true selves' (Miller 1988) as they go about the hard business of living, so also it is the goal for the professional development of the worker. Not a sterile, neutral role to be taught as a technology, the professional role is an alive one in the service of human-with-human relationship. Such a learning/teaching goal can be at odds with the dominant concerns of academe. Social work has the choice of being seduced by the technical–rational ethos of the university or continuously clarifying and developing the essentials of our kind of education for ourselves and our academic colleagues of other professional disciplines.

A study of a substantial number of psychotherapists (285 clinical psychologists) who answered anonymously a questionnaire about their feelings towards their patients was reported in the *New York Times* (4 May 1993). '...beneath their professional mask of unflappability', nearly a third reported 'hating' at least one patient and 46 per cent said they had been angry enough at a patient to have done something which they later regretted. 'Large numbers of therapists surveyed said their training did not prepare them to deal effectively with strong feelings towards patients.' This is not introduced here to expose a related profession. The researchers feel that their findings could apply to any of the helping disciplines including social work. The findings can be seen as timely evidence of the critical importance of experiential learning in social work education and our need to protect it from pressure to conform to the technical–rationalism that thrives in the universities in which our education takes place.

When teaching social work learners in the field it is a stimulating experience to show a student how conceptual and theoretical knowledge can cast light on a practice situation, but also how a specific theory is rarely enough, since every human situation has its own uniqueness, can elude the theory and always requires a search for the meaning in the minds of those who are the recipients of service.

For the student working with groups, structural and dynamic theories of group processes are readily learned from the literature. However, the perceptual skill of tuning in to group process and assessing how the group as a whole is developing at the same time that one perceives what is happening to, within and among the individual members is a development of cognitive process that needs to be accomplished and practised experientially. So it is also with family work. To perceive and respond in terms of wholes and interacting parts is mental skill that should be required of every social worker, but cannot be developed simplistically as a technical–rational skill.

The task for social work educators and field instructors today is to continue the documentation and conceptualization of the experiential learning component of our professional education within academe and thus to contribute to an epistemology of practice.

Generalist practice and specialization

There is a critical dilemma for social work education because we, perhaps more so than any other human service profession, have a continuously broadening view of our mission as regards the human condition. Ours is a very large arena for scholarship and for practice skill. We view internal and external change to be valid. External reality can be as important a focus in the helping process as is the internal reality of the individual.

Let me be clear on the definition of social work practice from which I speak. Germain (1985) defines the central dimensions for social work intervention as 'practice ... directed towards improving the transactions between people and environments in order to enhance adaptive *and* improve environments for all who function within them' (p. 27). Vigilante (1981) defines the domain of social work as a psycho-social event at the interface between the individual and society. Falck (1985), endeavouring to conceptualize a holistic human behaviour base for social work practice by development of 'the membership perspective', defines social work practice as rendering professional aid in the management of membership (p. 56). Saleeby (1994), defining social work practice as 'meaning making' in people's lives, states that we cannot ignore the fact that 'we work at the intersection of self and social environment and the reality that somehow we have to work both sides of that street' (p. 357). Each of this sample of definitions assumes both internal and external change as appropriate directions for professional intervention.[5]

In the growing conceptualizations of this complex arena for social work activity, the earlier division of practice skill into three discrete methods, casework, group work and community work, was relatively simple. Reflecting historically on social work in North America, Bartlett (1970) pointed out how social work had been a profession of parts struggling for its wholeness (p. 22). The decades of the 1960s and 1970s, influenced by Bartlett and participated in by many of us, including myself (Papell 1978), constituted an era in which the profession of social work very directly and purposefully searched for its wholeness. Common, base, holistic, integrated, structural, ecological, systemic, and of course generic, were key words used in the conceptualizing and theory building of the profession that reflected the concern in that period with entirety rather than the 'growing parts'.

In order to make the historical picture of social work more complete we should remind ourselves that the word 'generic' first appeared in North American social work in the report of the Milford Conference (AASW 1929), but only a single method, namely case work, was then involved. At issue was the commonality of casework as a method wherever it might be practised. The recommendation was that the education presented in the university was to be generic while the specialized knowledge needed in settings wherever casework was practised – such as psychiatric, medical, child welfare – was to be taught in the field. There flowed from this decision the fundamental view of the terminal degree in social work as a generic beginning credential rather than a specialized one.

In North American social work in the 1960s, the thrust towards wholeness was of a different order from the generic issue of 1929. The other methods, group work and community organization, had burgeoned during and following World War II. The holistic and systemic notions were now taking into account that change in any part of human situations and systems could well be brought about by other than the one-on-one methodology. Thus a social worker, as a problem solver with humans in their societal predicaments, should be able to select and offer skilled service in the most viable methodology for the particular situation. After years of struggle to define terms and to weigh the multi-method notion, a generalist practice appears now to stand as a legitimate educational outcome for social work education at the BSW and first-year MSW levels, and an advanced generalist practice at the final MSW level if a school so opts (CSWE 1991; Schatz, Jenkins and Sheafor 1990; Tolson, Reid and Garvin 1994).

Despite the validation of a generalist practice, the more expectable curriculum model in North American social work education is a foundation BSW and first MSW year, with concentration or specialization in the second MSW year (CSWE 1991). The wholeness of the complex professional domain that is social work does not readily stay in place in our curricular designs. We have not solved the educational challenge that social work practice calls for. Rather, the contemporary era seems to be characterized by a thrust again towards a new/old kind of specialization, now in relation to fields of practice, settings, populations or social problems, in North America carefully labelled 'concentration' at the MSW level (CSWE 1991).

Why is it so difficult for this profession and its educators to hold to the wholeness in social work practice? It is not that human problems are any greater (although I suspect that in the 1990s many of us have had to give up our earlier illusions that it would be possible for society to be less toxic for humankind than it seems to be). Perhaps it is because knowledge has become so vast, and certainly not less important. As an example, new knowledge about relapse is necessary for social workers in the field of addictions in helping the recovering person and the people in his/her world that are assaulted by the illness.

I must state my position clearly. I believe that the generic knowledge of the helping process, based upon the methodological development of which our profession can be amply proud, is neither easily learned nor readily integrated into skill in the helping role. Rather than struggling to solve the problem of such a complex educational task, North American social work has grasped at specialization for the entry MSW level of practice. This is a trend that can be viewed as pressure away from the ideology, humanism and wholeness of the social work mission. Specialization should be a *post-Masters* educational undertaking and a continuing educational goal for professional social workers. This does not mean that a BSW or MSW curriculum cannot include lively and important courses on issues, problems and settings. But it does mean that the concept of specialization for our profession should contain a depth and achievement well beyond the entry level degree.

An example of the urgency of adequate methodological education in the curriculum is found in recent research. Steinberg (1992) has shown that there is a difference in the work with groups done by social work practitioners who have had group work education (three semesters) and those who have not. The difference, studied in relation to the worker's thinking process about control in the group, seemed to lie in his/her understanding and skill in developing mutual aid. Practitioners *without* group work education tended to use voting rather than consensus as the modus operandi for helping the group to reach decisions. They tended to regard interpersonal conflict as an unwelcome interruption to the real work of the group, an impediment and threat to the stability, rather than a normal consequence of group life and a legitimate aspect of process (pp. 12, 15). Practitioners *with* group work education routinely referred to stages of group development in framing their expectations; those *without* group work education appeared to have much less understanding of how 'use of self' would be influenced by time phases in a group process and of the concept of the development of the group over time (p. 16). It is also possible that a comparable difference would be found in studying the one-on-one work of social work professionals who have had a solid methodological education in casework and those who have not.

In whatever way the social work curriculum is designed, as it accommodates to the pressures for specialization, it must give ample priority to the essentials of social work's splendid achievements in the knowledge of practice and the development of methodological skill. Generically, every social work student should have substantial mastery of skill in the various units of practice upon completing the MSW entry degree.

Theoretical knowledge and the nature of the real world

There seems to me to be a common thread in these three issues for social work education, namely the question of knowledge, what it is, its exponential nature, and what to do with it, a problem that we surely share with all professions and disciplines in today's world.

I have stated that the dialectical nature of this particular issue, theory and the real world of humankind, stems from both within the profession and outside.[6] Perhaps some of you remember a few years ago when a debate was held by living Nobel Prize scholars. The question was whether knowledge will be able to save the world. The prestigious remarks from both sides of the question were both haunting and disturbing.

Thoughts on kinds of knowledge and knowing that are legitimate and vital to our particular profession and helpful to the learning/teaching enterprise are frequently noted in the literature (see for example: Hartman 1990; Pardeck, Murphy and Choi 1994; Papell 1992; Imre 1982; Goldstein 1993). The notion of 'practice wisdom' has appeared often in the practice language of our profession. Yet it is seldom listed in the indices of our text books. Let us consider how it might be defined. Certainly it has represented a way of saying that a social worker will need to use his/her own judgement at many moments when knowledge is not available to tell one what to do. An assumption is of course that the knowledge might have been available if the worker had had the time to search it out. Another assumption also might be that someday the knowledge will be available if we become scientific enough to discover it. A fear might be that the judgement of social workers is a subjective one and we are really do-gooders!

I would like to render a discussion of the concept of practice wisdom with a bit more admiration for what it takes to be a social worker and with a bit more humility about the human condition and the nature of knowledge about it. Whereas it is often possible to use knowledge to predict and therefore to determine outcome there is always a limitation on that prediction. The limitation is that all humans are travelling into their own future – that is the nature of the living process. It is *as* possible that the next moment *cannot* be known as it is that it can be predicted. Furthermore, life offers events which neither we nor our clients can plan or control. If the social worker's mind's eye is attuned to the reality that our clients are always moving into the unknown and their destiny is not the helper's to determine, then judgement, intuition, trusting one's instinct, wisdom become dignified and professional. It occurs to me that even the concept of the 'life model' (Germain and Gitterman 1980) becomes more understandable with such a mental approach. Working with strengths and respecting human decisions and frailty, including one's own, become more acceptable and we avoid becoming locked into 'pathologizing'. This approach to knowledge can be taught to social work students, in class and in field, in many ways as they struggle with the painful life processes of their profession's complex societal mission.

Social work students are taught that there is knowledge that will help them in their work and that as professionals they will have a responsibility to participate in generating knowledge. But do we teach them enough about the use of knowledge, that no knowledge can do more than inform their thinking and illuminate the situation for them? Social work learners must perceive the human situation which they confront in their practice and recognize that their perceptions are filtered through their own thinking and knowing processes, through their own emotions and feeling processes and through the way they themselves integrate and regulate their own doing or behaving. Knowing the self is more than knowing how one feels. It is also knowing how one thinks and how one acts. The heuristic paradigm and constructionist epistemology can be helpful in the education of social work learners about professional knowledge and knowing. While this is important content for the academic courses, nowhere can it be better explicated and experienced than in the practicum as the students involve themselves in the life space of their clients and become for a moment participants in the clients' life journey.

In summary

In addressing these three compelling issues in education for the social work profession, experiential learning in academe, specialization in a profession that demands a holistic perspective, and the mind at work in professional human encounters, I find guidelines for reflective practice and teaching. If the issues have only been introduced, I have tried to do so in the context of my own points of view, my own heuristics, trusting that you who are also compelled by this profession will hear my particular biases even as you continue to participate in the discourse into the future.

An afterthought

Today I have taken some time off from writing about social work education to work in my garden. It is not precisely planful. One never knows what will come up and where. So in the spring I protect some plants from intrusion; I develop boundaries between various prolific seeders that would take over the entire garden if allowed; I weed out a brown-eyed susan that has come up in the irises. I was stunned to find that something I had planted last year is coming back again this year plentifully.

I think to myself that this is what I am writing about, my world view. I could not have known what would happen this year. Life has taken charge in my garden and aspects of it are beyond my imagination!

Then I talk further to myself. Maybe I *could* have known that whatever it was that I planted would reseed. Maybe I *should* have known! But I did not! As the gardener it is my pleasure to find something unexpected and very viable in the living processes in my garden, and to help them along. I can help but I cannot do the growing and the life process is far beyond my control.

I talk further to myself. This is my style of gardening; planning a more disciplined predictable design for a garden and knowing everything possible about the plant before you put it in is just as good a style as mine, as long as the living process is handled tenderly and respected.

I think to myself that it probably does not matter what are the styles of the social work curriculum designers and teachers around these educational issues that have been on my mind. If our students as professional helpers are taught to reflect about the issues in relation to their engagements with humans, possibly the resolutions of the issues are irrelevant!

Notes

1   Based on a paper presented at the Director's Luncheon, School of Social Work, Memorial University of Newfoundland, 12 May 1993.

2   See Grinell, R.M., Jr *et al.* (43 signatures) (1994), Social Work Researchers' Quest for Respectability. The signers are challenging Tyson's critique of the positivist paradigm (1992).

3   See also Tyson, K. 'Author's reply: Response to "Social Work Researchers" Quest for Respectability' (1994).

4   For example, an entire issue of *Journal of Teaching in Social Work* edited by Laird 1993, brings together a number of social work scholar-educators who have been using postmodern and social constructionist epistemological lenses for social work theory building in their own practice, research and teaching (p. 1).

5   I am reminded by my colleague Professor Jerome Sachs (personal correspondence, 1993) that any effort at defining social work practice must always include directly a recognition of the profession's values and objectives re: social justice. Likewise, the practitioner's reflective process, while accepting that the mind affects and even 'constructs' the perceptions of reality, is obligated to contain social work's professional commitment to a more fair and more equitable world for our clients and all humankind.

6   For a discussion of this field of neurology, see *A Leg to Stand On* by Oliver Sacks, MD.

References

American Association of Social Workers (1929), *Social Case Work Generic and Specific: A Report of the Milford Conference.* New York: AASW. Reprinted by National Association of Social Workers, Silver Spring, MD: 1974.

Bartlett, H.M. (1970), *The Common Base of Social Work Practice.* New York: National Association of Social Workers, Inc.

Council on Social Work Education (1991), *Handbook of Accreditations Standards and Procedures.* New York: CSWE.

Falck, H.S. (1985), *Social Work: The Membership Perspective.* New York: Springer Publishing Company.

Germain, C.B. (1985), 'Introduction: Ecology and social work', in C.B. Germain (ed.), *Social Work Practice: People and Environments.* New York: Columbia University Press.

Germain, C.B. and Gitterman, A. (1980), *The Life Model of Social Work Practice.* New York: Columbia University Press.

Goldstein, H. (1993), 'The Search for Subjugated Knowledge Reconsidered', *Social Work,* **38** (5), 643–5.

Grinell, R.M. Jr *et al.* (1994), 'Social Work Researchers' Quest for Respectability', *Social Work,* **39** (4), 469–71.

Hartman, A. (1990), 'Many Ways of Knowing', *Social Work,* **35**, 3–4.

Hartman, A. (1992), 'In Search of Subjugated Knowledge', *Social Work,* **37** (6), 483–4.

Imre, R. (1982), *Knowing and Caring: Philosophical Issues in Social Work.* Lanham, MD: University Press of America, Inc.

Laird, J. (ed.) (1993), 'Revisioning Social Work Education: A social constructionist approach', *Journal of Teaching in Social Work,* entire issue, **8** (1/2).

Miller, Alice (1987), *The Drama of the Gifted Child.* New York: Basic Books, Inc.

Moustakas, C. (1990), *Heuristic Research: Design, Methodology and Applications.* Newbury Park, CA: Sage Publications, Inc.

New York Times, (1993), 'Some patients arouse hatred, therapists find', May 4 p. C11.

Papell, C.P. (1978), 'Teaching the technology of social work: cumulative methods to unitary whole', in K. Dea (ed.), *New Ways of Teaching Social Work Practice,* New York: CSWE.

Papell, C.P. (1992), 'Groupwork with new populations: knowledge and knowing', in J. Garland (ed.), *Groupwork Reaching Out: People, Places and Power.* New York: Haworth Press.

Papell, C.P. and Skolnik, L. (1992), 'The Reflective Practitioner: A Contemporary Paradigm's Relevance for Social Work Education', *Journal of Social Work Education,* **28** (1), 18–26.

Pardeck, J.T., Murphy, J.W. and Choi Jung Min (1994), 'Some Implications of Postmodernism for the Social Work Practice', *Social Work,* **39** (4), 343–6.

Sacks, O. (1990), *A Leg to Stand On.* New York: Harper-Collins Publishers.

Saleeby, D. (1994), 'Culture, Theory, and Narrative: The Intersection of Meaning in Practice', *Social Work,* **39** (4), 351–59.

Schatz, M.S., Jenkins, L.E. and Sheafor, B.W. (1990), 'Milford Redefined: A Model of Initial and Advanced Generalist Social Work', *Journal of Social Work Education,* **26** (54), 217–31.

Schön, D.A. (1983), *The Reflective Practitioner.* New York: Basic Books, Inc.

Schön, D.A. (1987), *Educating the Reflective Practitioner.* San Francisco: Jossey Bass.

Sherman, E. and Reid, W.J. (eds) (1994), *Qualitative Research in Social Work.* New York: Columbia University Press.

Steinberg, D.M. (1992), 'Some Findings from a Study on the Impact of Group Work Education on Social Work Practitioners' Work with Groups', *Social Work With Groups*, **16** (3), 23–40.

Tolson, E.R., Reid, W.J. and Garvin, C.D. (1994), *Generalist Practice: A Task-Centred Approach*. New York: Columbia University Press.

Tyson, K.B. (1992), 'A New Approach to Relevant Scientific Research for Practitioners: The Heuristic Paradigm', *Social Work*, **37** (6), 541–56.

Tyson, K. (1994), 'Author's Reply: Response to "Social Work Researchers" Quest for Respectability', *Social Work*, **39** (6), 737–41.

Vigilante, J.L. (1981), 'Searching for Theory: Following Hearn'. Presented at Annual Program Meeting, Council on Social Work Education, Louisville, Kentucky, March 1981.

3 Course design for reflective practice

David Boud and Susan Knights

The importance of a reflective approach to practice has been emphasized in many professions in recent years. Donald Schön's *The Reflective Practitioner* (1983) drew attention to the fact that professional competence involves more than the application of technical expertise; not a new idea but one which had, up till then, little apparent influence on the design of university courses for the professions. Since the early 1980s there has been a great deal of discussion about educating reflective practitioners particularly in professions such as teaching, nursing and social work where field experience and academic course work need to be closely integrated (Schön 1987; Zeichner and Liston 1987; Korthagen 1988; Clift, Houston and Prignach 1990; Palmer, Burns and Bulman 1994; Smith and Hatton 1993). Such discussion has emphasized the importance of focusing on the artistry of practice and, within courses, of creating opportunities for students to engage in activities which promote reflective practice.

Independently of the work influenced by Schön there has been an increasing interest in the role of reflection in learning from experience and how reflective activities can be incorporated into learning in a variety of ways (Boud, Keogh and Walker 1985; Mulligan and Griffin 1992). There have been two separate emphases in this: the first on reflection which takes place alongside action, which has close parallels with Schön, the second on reflection which takes place following action. The latter has emerged from a group work tradition and from an interest in debriefing complex events.

The argument of this chapter is that the encouragement of reflective practice requires more than the development of effective ways of debriefing periods of field work or introducing a new topic into the curriculum; it requires finding appropriate ways to build notions of reflective practice into the processes of teaching and learning throughout courses.

Some current strategies

There are now many strategies which have come to be identified as contributing to reflection, for example, the use of learning journals and learning partners, debriefing activities, critical incident analysis, autobiographical work, the creation of concept maps, action research and various forms of computer-based dialogue (Boud, Keogh and Walker 1985; Holly 1989; Rosenthal 1991; Zeichner 1986). While these methods, if not common, are at least familiar in higher education, their use now is being more clearly conceptualized as having the purpose of 'turning experience into learning' (Boud, Keogh and Walker 1985) or offering students the opportunity to process their experience to generate alternative ways of viewing a situation and achieving new appreciations or understandings. While each of these approaches has a particular focus, they share the feature that students are encouraged to return to their own experiences in class and outside and focus on what these events mean to them.

The following are examples of strategies used in our own teaching. The context here is one of courses for mature students who are already practitioners in the field of adult education.

Learning journals

Students are required to keep a weekly journal in which they record and comment on their experience as learners in the course (what kinds of activities do they enjoy? what gets in the way of their learning? how does their experience relate to the theory they are hearing and reading about?). Five minutes at the end of the class time is devoted to journal writing. For some students this is all they need, others use this as a beginning and write more during the week, sometimes a great deal more. At the end of the semester students review their journal entries and submit an overview of their learning about themselves as adult learners and ways in which they think this might influence their own practice as adult educators (Knights 1991). In other courses this idea is extended and students are encouraged to keep other forms of personal–professional journals (Holly 1989), dialogue journals (Reinertsen and Wells 1993) or learning portfolios (Bawden and McKinnon 1980; Walker 1985; Barnett and Lee 1994; MacIsaac and Jackson 1994).

Learning partners

Students are introduced to the idea of using a learning partner at the beginning of a course. They are encouraged, though not required, to choose another member of the class to act as their partner. The aim of this relationship is for each student to have someone else with whom they discuss ideas that are raised, explore their own interests, exchange work for comment and generally to be a friendly person upon whom they can call (Robinson, Saberton and Griffin 1985). (The importance of a listener in supporting individual reflection is discussed in detail in Knights 1985.) The formalization of this arrangement is particularly important for busy part-time students who often do not have the same opportunities for peer interaction as those who are less pressured by family and work commitments. Students are encouraged to meet for coffee, for example, and then make their own arrangements which might involve telephone contact or meeting briefly before or after class. Support for learning partnerships as a reflective activity is indicated by Smith and Hatton's (1993) research on the measurement of reflection which suggests that more reflection may occur with 'critical friends' than through interaction with staff or through written assignments.

Use of learning contracts

The widespread use of contract learning at all levels means that learning tasks which are meaningful to each student are negotiated with staff members and through this process students become committed to them (Knowles 1975; Anderson, Boud and Sampson forthcoming). This form of tailoring courses and subjects to individual needs is a form of 'liberating structure' (Torbert 1978) that provides a framework in which students can operate, but which does not unilaterally define the specific features of learning tasks in which they engage. The use of contracts prompts reflection at three stages: prior to the preparation of an initial draft to be submitted to a staff member students need to focus on their experiences, their learning needs and how they might pursue them; in dialogue with staff their conceptions of these are challenged and a revised contract produced; and prior to final submission of the outcomes of their learning students are prompted by the contract to review their learning and how they can present it to another person. The use of contracts is ubiquitous in our School and is the predominant form of assessment in most courses. Strong support for them among both staff and students at all levels has been found (Anderson, Boud and Sampson 1994).

Self-assessment schedules

One of the difficulties of conventional assignments in promoting reflection is that they tend to concentrate on relatively few aspects of a course. Self-assessment schedules are used as a means of enabling students to bring together a wide range of their learning in a course, to reflect on their achievements and to examine the implications for further learning. A completed schedule is a document in which students are required to identify the objectives they have been pursuing during a course (their own and others, predetermined and emergent), establish criteria for judging the achievement of these objectives, explain what evidence they have which will demonstrate their achievements (written work, contributions to class, notes on readings, feedback from others, etc.), make judgements about the extent and quality of their achievements and report on what further action they need to engage in (if any) with respect to any of the objectives which they have set (Boud 1992). Such a schedule fits well with the keeping of learning journals.

While these four approaches promote reflection, they also have features which address other desired objectives. Reflection is not something independent of what students are otherwise expected to learn and reflective practices are not separate from the normal teaching and learning practices of a course. It is often desirable to build reflective elements into activities which serve other teaching values and content objectives. Thus, in the examples given above, learning journals are a way of students keeping a record of their learning, learning partners have a peer support function as well as encouraging reflection, learning contracts are a way of organizing and keeping track of learning activities, and self-assessment schedules can be used as one element of formal assessment. In each case students are working with the substantive content of the course.

Most conceptualizations of reflection and reflective teaching are based on logical and analytical ways of information processing, but there are other ways of interpreting data and making decisions which make use of 'gestalts'. Korthagen (1993) proposes a broader form of reflection and reflective teaching than is often discussed which includes the mental 'mirroring' of these non-rational processes and argues for the importance of integrating the rational and non-rational in reflection. Strategies of this type include the use of metaphors, drawing or painting, making photographs, guided fantasies and Kelly's repertory grid.

Models of reflection

Reflection as a term is used in a number of different ways by different authors. We take our definition from Boud, Keogh and Walker (1985) as 'a generic term for those intellectual and affective activities in which individuals engage to explore their experiences in order to lead to new understandings and appreciations' (p. 19). They developed a three-stage model of the reflection process focusing on: returning to the experience, attending to feelings connected with the experience and re-evaluating the experience through recognizing implications and outcomes.

This model has subsequently been extended into a model for facilitating learning from experience (Boud and Walker 1990; Boud 1993). The essence of this model is that learning from experience can be enhanced through both reflection-in-action, that is reflection which occurs in the midst of experience, and through reflection after an event (reflection-on-action). Both forms of reflection can be introduced into courses, though in different ways.

The features of the model include the following: reflection is grounded in the personal foundation of experience of the learner, that is, those experiences which have shaped the person and have helped to create the person he or she is now, and their intent which gives a particular focus to their learning in any particular context. Learning occurs through the interaction of the person with his or her material and human environment – the learning milieu – and is assisted through the learner giving attention to noticing what is happening in themselves and in their external environment, intervening in various ways to influence themselves and the milieu in which they are operating and reflecting-in-action continually to modify their noticing and interventions. The model suggests that there are an endless number of reflective strategies which might be adopted, but those which are chosen must be related to the needs and intent of the learner and the nature of the milieu.

Although the model was originally developed in the context of non-accredited (though deliberate) learning, it has also been applied elsewhere. In the context of university courses, the curriculum and the teacher are strong elements in the learning milieu (see Figure 1).

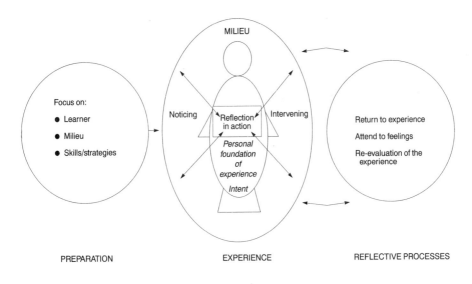

Figure 1   Model for promoting learning from experience

Designing for reflection

The illustrations of reflective activities given earlier are just a few of many possibilities. Exercises and learning activities which are currently used as a normal part of a course can be designed or redesigned with a view to enhancing those features which contribute to promoting reflection. Reflection is about something and it occurs in a particular context; it must always be considered as an element of an overall design which links with the learning goals and curriculum content of a course. While some activities, such as keeping a journal, have become identified as reflective, it is not useful to talk about reflective devices independent of the context in which they are to be used.

While there are some activities like those mentioned previously which have reflection as a dominant characteristic, it is important to identify those features of any learning activity which are likely to promote students' reflection. The following indicates some of these features which flow from the model of facilitating learning from experience discussed above:

- Learners are actively engaged with a task which they accept is for learning (they are not simply following a prescription or set of rules, but are contributing their own thinking to the task).
- The task is constructed to allow significant elements of choice by the learners so that they can begin to own it and make it meaningful and worthwhile for them – it thus becomes a task which is not undertaken simply to satisfy the needs of the teacher.
- The event is not totally predictable to the participants and learners are prompted to notice what they did not expect.
- Learners' experience is challenged or confronted in some way which allows them to reassess their experience and the assumptions on which they are operating.
- Learners are obliged to intervene in some way in their own learning process; they have to make choices and follow the consequences of their choices.
- Learners are required to link what is new to them to their existing frameworks of understanding or confront the need to modify these frameworks.

Reflection in the sense used here is a conscious act of the learner. It is not meaningful to think of 'going through the motions' of reflection even though many students will respond instrumentally in this manner when confronted with a requirement to do so. Setting an assignment which the staff member believes will encourage reflection is not sufficient; the intent of the student is crucial as most activities can be turned into ones in which the semblance of reflection can be portrayed.

Learning activities may promote different types and degrees of reflection. While it may be difficult to distinguish reliably between what is and is not a reflective task, it is possible to introduce features into an activity which increase the likelihood of it becoming a reflective one. For example, when students engage in a self-assessment exercise on an assignment, they are more likely to approach it reflectively if they are expected to take each aspect in turn and make a judgement about their own work with respect to that aspect rather than making a global judgement about their overall work. They are also more likely to approach it reflectively when they are expected to write a phrase or sentence about each aspect, rather than give a numerical rating for each. A similar approach can be used in student evaluations of teaching. Asking students to complete open-ended sentences ('my major learning from this subject was . . .', 'my main difficulty in learning in this subject was . . .' and so on) or give other qualitative assessments of their learning in the subject is likely to promote reflection about their experience and learning in the course whereas the assignment of a number on a scale from one to five simply provides the lecturer with (dubious) quantitative data.

Creating a context for reflection

These points underline the importance of introducing and establishing an effective climate for reflection, and this is inextricably linked with establishing an effective climate for learning more generally. All learning requires learners actively to engage with knowledge, but reflection makes such engagement an essential part of the process.

Our experience suggests that the following are important in introducing and establishing a productive climate for reflection:

- *Articulating an educational rationale for the process.* Why is reflection important, why bother with it? How is it different from other aspects of learning, particularly memorizing and problem solving? It may be useful to introduce students to the idea of different levels of reflection. Van Manen (1977), for example, discusses three different levels: the first concerned with techniques needed to reach given objectives, the second concerned with clarifying assumptions and assessing the consequences of different actions and the third concerned with principles such as justice, equity and human concerns.
- *Introducing a simple exercise to illustrate reflection.* For example, asking students in pairs to interview each other about an activity earlier in the class using the reflective questions: what happened? How do you feel? What does it mean?

- *Providing an opportunity for students to clarify their understanding of the idea.* Making the distinction between reflection and evaluation or record keeping, or reflective and non-reflective thinking and encouraging students to bring forward examples and non-examples of reflection to be discussed.

- *Introducing a framework or model to aid thinking about elements of reflection.* For example, by referring to that of Boud and Walker (1990) or some aspect thereof.

- *Modelling a reflective approach in one's own presentation of the idea.* If the idea is presented as instructions to be followed, it will contradict the notion of reflection that is being promoted. The staff member must plan for, expect and allow for considerable questions and discussion and must treat the issues raised in a thoughtful way, engaging with them rather than offering an immediate technical response. Particular attention needs to be given to wait-time (Tobin 1987) so that the learners feel that the staff member has made some attempt to reflect upon their concerns and respond to them, rather than presenting the plan as a fait accompli.

- *Identifying areas of the process that students can make their own.* Reflection cannot be determined exclusively by staff and students have to bring an agenda of their own which they pursue in the process.

- *Providing time.* Reflection takes time and it will normally considerably occupy students outside the class. The importance of it can be emphasized if the staff member commits class time to reflective activities particularly at the early stages. This will demonstrate that the teacher takes the matter seriously and is willing to allocate precious meeting time to an important matter. Later in a semester, very small amounts of class time can be very productively used for reflection, for example, in having students complete a one-minute paper or reflection on the topic of the class at the end of the session.

- *Treating reflection as a normal activity.* While it might be necessary to build particular reflection activities into courses in a way which at first might seem a little self-conscious, the aim is for them to become commonplace over time and be regarded as part of the norm of teaching and learning. This is a positive development if it means that the ideas of reflection are being internalized by all parties involved, but it is not if reflection becomes a ritual which is conducted in a non-reflective manner!

Reflective activities in themselves cannot compensate for courses which are not related to the concerns of the student, nor ones in which students are so overloaded that they cannot take each task on its merits and engage fully with it. The reviewing of courses to ensure that they are generally realistic needs to proceed alongside considerations of enhancing the place of reflection in them.

Assessment and reflection

Although the role of assessment and grading in relation to reflective activities is problematic, it seems to us that in an environment where other aspects of learning are assessed, relating reflection to assessment requirements in some way appears to be necessary. The question is what kind of evidence can students be expected to provide to indicate that they have been engaged in reflection, how can this evidence be collected without inhibiting the very processes which we are seeking to encourage and how should this be assessed?

In our courses assessment tasks have taken the form of the presentation of written reports of the outcomes of reflective activities such as self-assessment schedules, overviews of journals or reports of self-monitoring. Since reflection is a very individual activity, based, as described above, on the personal foundation of the experience of the learner, we believe it is inappropriate to grade reflection in a way which suggests that one student's reflection is of more value than another's. This does not imply that we believe there are no qualitative differences in different examples of reflection. There is also a danger that grading might lead to students trying to impress an assessor and gain higher marks for a 'correct' response which means that they are unlikely to focus on a central aspect of reflection: exploring their uncertainties and considering alternative or creative ways of viewing the material with which they are working.

What is sought in considering reflective reports is evidence that the learner can give an account of a particular experience, be aware of any emotional response the activity engendered and describe the outcomes of reflecting on the experience such as new awareness ('I realized that as a learner I felt very uncomfortable without a clearly defined structure to each session'), decisions ('I decided that I would in future make sure to provide this for my own students'), new questions ('I noticed that fellow students experienced this activity in a very different way and feel I need to test my conclusions again') or new understanding ('looking back on my journal entry for the first night of the course I realize how uncertain even adult students are at the beginning of any new learning activity'). Such reflective reports can only meaningfully be judged on a satisfactory/unsatisfactory basis where 'unsatisfactory' (or 'incomplete' if there is an opportunity to re-submit) would be applied to reports which simply tell the story or evaluate an activity with no evidence of the student working with or extracting learning from the experience.

Concluding thoughts

In writing about reflection we are conscious that we are dealing with a topic which has attained the status of being 'a good thing' and something which some teachers regard as self-evidently worthwhile. We believe that it is important and that reflective activities should be incorporated more effectively into courses. However, we are also conscious that reflection is a more problematic concept than is generally considered and that there is a need for critical debate about the nature of reflection, its role in learning and its inclusion in university courses. Unless we can be clear about how we can recognize reflection, how we can judge the effectiveness of any given reflective activity and create a suitable language for discussing reflection in learning we will not be able to develop the full potential of what we regard as an important component in the development of reflective practice. The literature on the subject is growing rapidly, but a lot more systematic work is required before we can be really confident that the particular practices currently being adopted are having the influences we desire.

Nevertheless, it is clear that course design must now take account of how students learn and the learning requirements of the professional practice for which they are being prepared. While such matters will be subject to deliberation by teaching staff, it is vital that these discussions be based upon good evidence. Although there is not a great deal of research on these matters in the specific area of social work education, the best we have to date from related areas indicates that it is prudent to structure courses around the idea that students are being prepared to become reflective practitioners and that opportunities for students to develop reflective skills and sensibilities should be embedded as a normal part of all professional courses.

Note

This chapter is a revised and extended version of a paper originally presented at the 1993 Annual Conference of the Higher Education Research and Development Society of Australasia at the University of New South Wales. It appeared in the conference proceedings as Boud, D. and Knights, S. (1994). 'Designing Courses to Promote Reflective Practice', *Research and Development in Higher Education*, **16**, 229–34.

References

Anderson, G., Boud, D. and Sampson, J. (1994), 'Expectations of Quality in the Use of Learning Contracts', *Capability: The International Journal of Capability in Higher Education* **1** (1), 22–31.

Anderson, G., Boud D. and Sampson, J. (forthcoming), *Learning Contracts: A Practical Guide*, London: Kogan Page.

Barnett, B. G. and Lee, P. (1994), 'Assessment processes and outcomes: building a folio', in L. Jackson & R. S. Caffarella (eds), *Experiential Learning: A New Approach. New Directions for Adult and Continuing Education* No. 62, San Francisco: Jossey Bass, pp. 55-62.

Bawden, R. and McKinnon, C. (1980), 'The Portfolio', *HERDSA News* (Higher Education Research and Development Society of Australasia), **2** (2), 4–5.

Boud, D. (1992), 'The Use of Self-assessment Schedules in Negotiated Learning', *Studies in Higher Education*, **17** (2), 185–200.

Boud, D. (1993), 'Experience as the Base for Learning', *Higher Education Research and Development*, **12** (1), 33–44.

Boud, D. and Walker, D. (1990), 'Making the Most of Experience', *Studies in Continuing Education*, **12** (2), 61–80.

Boud, D., Keogh, R. and Walker, D. (eds) (1985), *Reflection: Turning Experience into Learning*. London: Kogan Page.

Clift, R.T., Houston, R.W. and Prignach, M.C. (eds) (1990), *Encouraging Reflective Practice in Education: An Analysis of Issues and Programs*. New York: Teachers College Press.

Holly, M.L. (1989), *Writing to Grow: Keeping a Personal-Professional Journal*. Portsmouth, New Hampshire: Heinemann.

Knights, S. (1985), 'Reflection and learning: the importance of a listener', in D. Boud, R. Keogh and D. Walker (eds), *Reflection: Turning Experience into Learning*. London: Kogan Page, pp. 85–90.

Knights, S. (1991), 'Reflection and empowerment in the professional development of adult educators', in J. Mulligan and C. Griffin (eds) (1991), *Empowerment through Experiential Learning*. London: Kogan Page, pp. 170–77.

Knowles, M.S. (1975), *Self-directed Learning: A Guide for Learners and Teachers*. New York: Association Press.

Korthagen, F. (1988), 'The influence of learning orientations on the development of reflective teaching', in J. Calderhead (ed.), *Teachers' Professional Learning*. London: Falmer Press, pp. 35–50.

Korthagen, F.A.J. (1993), 'Two Modes of Reflection', *Teaching and Teacher Education*, **9** (3), 317–26.

MacIsaac, D. and Jackson, L. (1994), 'Assessment processes and outcomes: portfolio construction', in L. Jackson and R.S. Caffarella (eds), *Experiential Learning: A New Approach. New Directions for Adult and Continuing Education*, No. 62. San Francisco: Jossey-Bass, pp. 63–72.

Mulligan, J. and Griffin, C. (eds) (1992), *Empowerment through Experiential Learning*. London: Kogan Page.

Palmer, A., Burns, S. and Bulman, C. (eds) (1994), *Reflective Practice in Nursing: The Growth of the Professional Practitioner*. London: Blackwell Scientific.

Reinertsen, P.S. and Wells, M.C. (1993), 'Dialogue Journals and Critical Thinking', *Teaching Sociology*, **21**, 182–6.

Robinson, J., Saberton, S. and Griffin, V. (1985), *Learning Partnerships: Interdependent Learning in Adult Education*. Toronto: Department of Adult Education, Ontario Institute for Studies in Education.

Rosenthal, D.B. (1991), 'A Reflective Approach to Science Methods Courses for Preservice Elementary Teachers', *Journal of Science Teacher Education*, **2**, (1), 1–5.

Schön, D.A. (1983), *The Reflective Practitioner*. London: Temple Smith.

Schön, D.A. (1987), *Educating the Reflective Practitioner*. San Francisco: Jossey Bass.

Smith, D.L. and Hatton, N. (1993), 'Reflection in Teacher Education: a Study in Progress', *Educational Research and Perspectives*, **20** (1), 13–23.

Tobin, K. (1987), 'The Role of Wait Time in Higher Cognitive Level Learning', *Review of Educational Research*, **57** (1), 69–95.

Torbert, W.R. (1978), 'Educating Towards Shared Purpose, Self-direction and Quality Work: the Theory and Practice of Liberating Structure', *Journal of Higher Education*, **49** (2), 109–35.

Van Manen, M. (1977), 'Linking Ways of Knowing with Ways of Being Practical', *Curriculum Inquiry*, **6**, 205–28.

Walker, D. (1985), 'Writing and reflection', in D. Boud, R. Keogh and D. Walker (eds), *Reflection: Turning Experience into Learning*. London: Kogan Page, pp. 52–68.

Zeichner, K. (1986), 'Preparing Reflective Teachers: an Overview of Instructional Strategies which have been Employed in Preservice Teacher Education', *International Journal of Educational Research*, **11** (5), 565–75.

Zeichner, K. and Liston, D. (1987), 'Teaching Student Teachers to Reflect', *Harvard Educational Review*, **57** (1), 23–48.

4 Learning from experience and reflection in social work education

Alma Harris

Introduction

In recent years, there has been substantial research into student learning in higher education and much keen scrutiny of professional education. This work has looked at the different approaches novices use to undertake various learning tasks and at the outcomes of using these approaches on student learning (Marton and Saljo 1984; Saljo 1988; Marton and Ramsden 1987). In social work education, there have also been a number of recent influential studies which have looked particularly at the processes of teaching, learning and assessment in relation to supervision (Gray and Gardiner 1992; Gardiner 1984, 1989). In particular, there has been much interest in the relationship between theory and practice, as references to a 'gap between theory and practice' in social work are acknowledged to be 'common place' (Pilalis 1986, p. 79).

Within professional education, theory and practice are frequently regarded as separate entities. Often the former is viewed as primarily the responsibility of the college or university, which aims to build the theoretical knowledge of the student and the latter the responsibility of the clinic or hospital. In social work education, questions regarding the relevance of any theory to practice are a product of such separation (Chamberlain 1977; Hamilton 1981; Pearson 1975; Hearn 1982) and social workers agree that the nature of the relationship between theory and practice is problematic (Pilalis 1986). The conventional characterization of the cognitive processes involved in social work practice is that theory is selected and deductively applied to meet the contingencies of the case and the context of practice. Also, that the cognitive processes accompanying professional practice involve the deductive selection of a theoretical approach from a potential range of alternatives to meet the contingencies of the presenting situation (Gould 1989).

In essence, this separation between theory and practice underpins much professional training and in particular reflects the position within social work education. It has been argued that the 'theory into practice' perspective generates considerable confusion and dissatisfaction among students. Indeed surveys of social work students undertaken by Davies (1984) and Gibbs and Cigno (1986) found this to be the case. They discovered that many social work students were dissatisfied with their education and training and had doubts about its relevance for their practice. Other studies based on interviews with social workers reported by Carew (1979) and Corby (1982) indicated that little use was made by practitioners of the theoretical material taught on courses and that practitioners relied on 'home grown' wisdom. In this respect, students might more profitably be encouraged to understand 'theory through experience' or as Boud, Cohen and Walker (1993) have paraphrased it 'to treat the whole of experience as relevant' in professional learning (Boud, Cohen and Walker 1993, p. 86).

Experiential learning and reflection

It is suggested here that 'theory through experience' is not to advocate the abandonment of conventional social work theory, but instead to pursue a reconstructed conception and a more usable form of theory. It is suggested that that experiential learning theory and Schön's (1983) concept of 'reflection-in-action' offer an alternative epistemology which can be used by social work educators, practitioners and researchers within the field. The solution to the problem of fusing theory and practice using this model is essentially a procedural one. Students are confronted with experiences or phenomena which demand comment and explanation; their comments are then integrated by both peers and tutors in order to reach 'higher' levels of understanding.

A theoretical basis for this argument lies chiefly in a subscription to phenomenography. This theory argues that conceptual change is about a process, a searching for meaning, developing understanding and relating that understanding to the world around. Saljo (1979) identified five distinctively different conceptions of learning which he placed in a hierarchy which have been broadly replicated by other writers (Van Rossum and Schenk 1984; Marton and Ramsden 1987). It is claimed that such a categorization makes it possible to differentiate between surface and qualitative differences, which describe fundamental differences in the ways in which phenomena may be understood. Marton (1988) argues that qualitative differences are educationally critical because they are effective tools, capable of informing decisions about which teaching strategies are appropriate in helping students to develop any educationally preferred understanding (Marton and Saljo 1984).

In principle, these 'pedagogic procedures' are ones which, it is suggested, are likely to promote fundamental understanding. They are perfectly consistent, for example, with modern cognitivism which argues that most learning is essentially about modifying existing models of understanding, and that for this to happen tutors must first encourage students to reveal their current understanding, and then encourage them to discuss and 'experiment' so that those understandings can be challenged. Repertory grid technique has been one method employed with social work students specifically to explore the content of thinking about practice and to reveal students' current understanding (Gould 1991, 1993).

Schema theory has also been one means of describing how acquired knowledge is organized in the mind and how cognitive structures facilitate the use of knowledge in particular situations (Rumelhart 1980; Mezirow 1985). This theory argues that events are selected and organized into meaning schemas and that a range of factors can influence the meaning attached to an event which renders it significant. It is also argued that experiences (events) are used continually to enhance or diminish, endorse or reject meaning schemas and that through the process of reflection, new data continually influence and are influenced by existing schemas. This is the basis of learning from experience.

While writers like Kolb (1984) have done much to develop a coherent theory of experiential learning in the UK in the last five years, experiential learning remains a relatively uncharted area with little tradition of research (Boud and Walker 1990). Experiential learning can be defined as not merely abstract: it is the learning in which the learner is directly in touch with the realities being studied. One difficulty however, which has been highlighted with the models of experiential learning, is the fact that it does not discuss the nature of reflection in much detail and does not uncover the elements of reflection itself (Mezirow 1985, p. 13). It has been further suggested that the skill of experiential learning in which people tend to be most deficient is reflection (Mezirow 1985, p. 8) and that there are identifiable barriers to reflection (Boud, Cohen and Walker 1993; Boud, Keogh and Walker 1985).

While some professionals have the capacity for unsupported reflection, the majority will require some form of assistance. Similarly, while some professionals learn from every experience, others learn from selective experiences which possess certain characteristics or features. Despite all that has been written about reflection, it is therefore difficult to be precise about the nature of the process involved in reflection. Similarly, there is little empirical investigation of the processes involved in learning from practice (Syson and Baginsky 1981 and Gardiner 1989 are notable exceptions). Much of the literature on practice learning draws on adult learning theory which in turn is often both heuristic and *a priori*. As Collins (1989) observed most theories of learning are 'black boxish' and say little about the transformations involved in the learning process.

Within social work education, research has shown that tutors have an important role to play in helping students understand and refine the process of learning from experience. There has been little research, however, on the process and practice of experiential learning in social work education. As noted earlier, there is surprisingly little published research on the experience of beginning practice, or the relationship between practice and social work education. The research which does exist has sought from graduates their assessments of whether social work education had prepared them for practice (Shaw and Walton 1978; Stevenson and Parsloe 1978; Smith and Sandford 1980). There is less research evidence available which concentrates upon the types of experiences social work students have, and the way in which they reflect upon and learn from those experiences.

UFC Research Project

In 1991, funding was received from the University Funding Council to investigate experiential learning in higher education. The fields of social work and teaching were selected because of the central role of experience in professional development. The aims of the research were twofold: first, the project aimed to provide information about the way in which personal experience had shaped students' perceptions of professional training and, secondly, to explore the nature and type of students' learning experiences during placement.

The research was located theoretically within an interpretative paradigm informed by the phenomenological approach to social science, developed by Schutz and Wagner (1970). It sought to understand and interpret students' own perceptions of their experience. The method chosen was that of semi-structured interview which allowed respondents to describe and interpret their experiences relatively freely, within a broad framework constituted by the aims of the researcher. The research design was similar to the strategy advocated by Paley (1987) on the basis of his explorations into social work. The method employed in analysing the interview data was that of analytic induction. In the course of the analysis some patterns began to emerge from the students' accounts of their work, which taken together constituted a framework within which data was explained. The framework offered a multidimensional view of the students' experience from which generalizations and conclusions were made.

In the first phase the students were interviewed at the outset of their training and asked about their prior experiences and their views concerning professional development. This phase of the project focused primarily on the way in which personal experience had shaped students' conceptions of professional training. In the second phase, students were interviewed directly following a period of time spent on their practice placement, involving a wide range of agencies. The research investigated the type of learning experiences during placement and explored how learning from experience had taken place in practice. The remainder of the chapter will draw upon the findings from both of these phases in turn.

a) Pre-course phase

The literature on learning has shown that the characteristics and aspirations of the learner are the most important factors in the learning process. The response of the learner to new experience is determined significantly by past experiences, which have contributed to the ways in which the learner perceives the world. The way one person reacts to a given situation will not be the same as others and this becomes more obvious when learners from diverse backgrounds work together. The power of biography in influencing social work students' choice to enter the profession and in influencing their views of social work practice was clearly demonstrated in the interviews. Some students had experienced direct contact with an agency. This in turn had prompted them to consider or enter the profession.

> My sister had started a YTS scheme at the local probation office and I'd always been interested in crime and why people committed crimes. I went into the probation office and had a chat and got involved in social work through that I think.

> I started child minding and moved on to fostering, did voluntary work and became quite involved with Social Services. So a few years ago I decided that what I really wanted to do was to become a social worker.

> I had a crack at doing some voluntary work with psychiatric patients in hospital and that was OK. But I thought it would institutionalize me very quickly, so I thought perhaps not. I played around with that but I realized social work was where I wanted to be, preferably probation.

Other students described past life experiences where they felt that they were rehearsing for social work, in the respect that they had engaged in experiences which placed them in the role of helper or counsellor.

> There's one instance. A friend of mine accidentally overdosed and I thought I knew her very well but it turned out that there were lots of unknown family problems. In the end she did tell me after taking this accidental overdose. I thought at the time that it might have been deliberate, but it turned out not to be. She was in a very depressed state and so even if you think people have told you everything there might be something that's still bothering them that they haven't managed to

talk about. They can often take a long time to feel safe enough to talk about it. I felt I was placed in the role of counsellor even though I had no training to fall back on.

There was one friend I had whose marriage broke down and I was there for her to help her through her divorce. Her children were taken into care. She attempted suicide I don't know how many times. Things like that. And being around for her I suppose influenced me quite a bit.

I found that people were coming to me with their problems and asking for advice. I often didn't know the answer but acted on their behalf.

Many students described how they felt these situations had enabled them to 'rehearse' for social work by allowing them to 'practise' the skills of counselling and helping. In many incidences experiences like this had been sufficient to influence students to embark on social work as a career. The fact that some students believed that they had been practising certain skills necessary for social work suggests that they believe that such skills might be easily transferred into professional practice.

The research revealed that students held a rather simplistic and unproblematic view of professional development at the start of their training. The notions of 'rehearsal and practice' re-appear in their responses which tend to imply that they subscribed to a model of professional learning which is 'technicist'. The underlying assumption of the technicist view is that professional learning involves the acquisition of certain skills and procedures which if rehearsed and practised sufficiently well will result in a competent practitioner. If we are to challenge this technicist view, at the core of any social work education course there has to be opportunity for students to re-examine the basis for their images of social work and to acknowledge that previous notions of practising or rehearsing could be potentially limiting to their future professional development.

b) Post-placement phase

The post-placement phase concentrated on the types of learning experiences described by students, and the process of learning from experience. It has been suggested that for adult learners most events which precipitate reflection arise out of normal occurrences in one's life. This could be provoked by a feeling of loss of confidence in or disillusionment with one's existing situation. This was clearly demonstrated in the students' accounts of experiences they had learned from most during their placement. Some experiences were very much of the type where students described themselves as being 'thrown in the deep end'. For example,

I did a placement in a prison and it was supposed to be an observation for a course at university. I was there to observe the senior but I was running two wings and wrote full parole reports. He left me in charge of the whole office a couple of times as well, in charge of really difficult clients. I read the file that he handed me for one when the home probation officer was coming to visit someone to tell them that their wife didn't want them back when they were released in a month's time and when I read the file I thought 'Oh no'. It was a really violent person and I didn't know what he was doing leaving me in charge of that. The officers were really helpful there and for the month I was there it was a really good learning experience. I was thrown in at the deep end, so I had to get on and do it.

Other students similarly described quite shocking or frightening experiences, which they said had been very unpleasant but which they felt had also helped them to learn.

So there are things there I've learnt about myself. About practical things. I had a client, a young man and a young woman, married with lots of children, only 23. Five children. The things there that probably were never resolved. I had to see them through an 18-month probation. There was a two-year probation order and I picked it up in 18 months. I learned then how little I knew and how little I know. After the order the guy actually committed suicide. That was quite a while after the order. It depends how you perceive success. He went through the order and he didn't re-offend. His wife didn't have any more children. They were no worse off financially when I started to their situation when I finished. So I could argue that even what little I put in actually kept the system ticking. But that was the turning point.

In the hospital we had a guy who was extremely violent and violence no longer frightens me. Well it does frighten me but I don't run away from it. I have learnt how to contain the fear. I can always remember being left with a man in a small room this big. There was never any hint of violence and I think I learned from that. I'm sure most violence comes from the people who are dealing with the situation. It's just experience like this that I will draw upon.

A student who has had unpleasant experiences when exposed to similar experiences, may again experience the same feelings of discomfort. These can potentially interfere with the process of subject matter learning, as the student may become so preoccupied with emotional reactions that the new information presented by the experience is not clearly perceived. This emotional load can carry over into the learner's processing of the subject, and unless some way can be found of resolving these feelings there will be only limited learning of the content in question.

Reflection, Schön claims, gives rise to 'on the spot' experiment (Schön 1983, 1987). Thus the practitioner is characterized as an action researcher testing 'knowing in action' against the circumstances of the new case and modifying intervention if necessary, and moving by a series of experimental steps to a strategy which appears successful. Schön argues that this is not simply the process of trial and error as new ideas are not randomly tested out but rather reflection on each effort sets the stage for the next attempt. The experienced practitioner accumulates a repertoire of 'knowing in action' to respond to the new case with an exemplar from his/her stock of strategies until a new situation provokes the necessity of reflection to extend his or her existent knowing in action. When students were asked how they felt they had learned they described a number of strategies. Some felt they had learned through talking and asking questions.

> By talking about it I suppose, asking questions if I need to, reading around the subject. If I've taken notes, writing them up. Some people just take the notes and can go back months later and read them but I have to write them up.

Several students felt that exposure to an experience itself had been sufficient to enable them to learn.

> Just through experience basically. I'm a great believer that if you don't try things you'll never know what you can do. If you try and it's not a good experience, you still learn something.

Other students felt that being introduced to and revisiting their mistakes with practice teachers was an important part of the learning process.

> My practice teacher was really good because he allowed me to make mistakes and would help me address them and find solutions for next time. I'm confident that I'll be allowed to make mistakes and this is how I'll learn.

> I think I learn a lot from criticism, being able to feel safe to have people give criticism. From going back and going over events in your mind.

Boud, Cohen and Walker (1993) stress the importance of revisiting or 'returning to experience' in the process of learning from experience. They suggest that 'other people can provide an invaluable means of identifying the discrepancy or dilemma; they can often see what may be obvious, but which is too close for us to notice. By supportively drawing our attention to it they can help us learn from experience even when they do not see themselves in that role' (p. 85). In this respect, both college tutors and practice teachers have a crucial role to play in facilitating student reflection and experiential learning.

Conclusion

To conclude, it is suggested that practice teachers and tutors should recognize and utilize students' experiences more fully within the process of professional development. Instead of aspiring to a deductive, applicative mode of practice, it is suggested that there is much to be gained from getting students to reflect on their experiences and to apply their extended understanding to their future professional practice. As Gray and Gardiner (1992) argue, 'it is important to give attention not simply to the content of learning but also to the relationship between learning approaches and learning outcomes and to the conceptions of learning which underlie them' (p. 91). Similarly, Kelly (1955), in his personal construct theory, refers to the individual and unique perception of each person. Consequently, it is suggested that student schemas could be made much clearer and sharper through the use of a means of structured reflection on experience.

Research on the learning styles of social workers suggests that they are typically convergent and very close to the concrete end of the spectrum (Sims 1981). Such learners are likely to have considerable difficulty transferring knowledge to new situations or in their thinking, if they are not able to bring reflection to bear on their experience. While students cannot be forced to reflect, they can be offered a chance to recollect. A tutor may suggest that students may like the opportunity to consider some earlier experiences. The students may accept the opportunity, but in many cases their willingness to do so will be highly dependent on the cues and mechanisms contrived by the tutor. If they recognize the cue they will be more likely to engage in the process of reflection.

Research has shown that this can be achieved through the use of specific methods including discovery methods, case studies, carefully selected learning projects and various forms of writing and recording. For example, journals, diaries and records of experience have increasingly been used as a means of self-reflection in teacher education (Harris and Russ 1994; Holly 1989; Holly and McLoughlin 1989; James and Denley 1992). Similarly, autobiographical texts, action research and peer/supervisor support groups have been advocated as ways in which reflection can be facilitated. (Butt, Raymond and Yamagishi 1988; Gore and Zeichner 1990; Knowles 1991; Holly 1989; Holly and McLoughlin 1989).

As noted earlier, it has been argued that the skill of experiential learning in which people tend to be most deficient is reflection (Mezirow 1985, p. 8). Repertory grids can be a base for producing hard statistical results from phenomenological data, but an equally important purpose is for researcher and students to experience the reflection process itself. The untapped potential for using repertory grid techniques for studying how social workers think about aspects of practice is very considerable and through that process helping practitioners to develop their experiential learning and reflection in action (Gould 1989; Thomas and Harri-Augstein 1985). Such research is very much part of the 'new paradigm' (Reason and Rowan 1981) where research is undertaken with subjects as co-researchers rather than from the perspective of positivist research on subjects.

As stated at the start of the chapter, there is a growing awareness in social work education that practice competence cannot be understood simply as the application of theoretical knowledge to real-life practice. The limitations of an epistemology, based on this relationship, are well documented. The difficulty of such a crude epistemology lies in the fact that it fails to deal with the complexity of social work practice itself. It fails to acknowledge that theory often has to be mediated by the practitioner to make it relevant and useful. The student evidence has shown that individuals learn from reflecting upon experience and engaging in active learning. While some social work programmes are moving in this direction (Burgess and Jackson 1990), this unfortunately, is not a general trend.

Consequently, it is suggested that experiential learning theory characterizes both an alternative epistemology and an alternative way of considering professional development in social work education. This process of learning gives access to the students' world view, and requires that educators engage with learners in the process of articulating and examining those assumptions, or constructs, which bear on their practice. Instead of arising out of academic theory, there is a shift in emphasis towards personal theorizing and exploring constructs culled directly from students' experience. If students are to move towards more complex and coherent models of practice, it would seem that social work education programmes premised on this alternative epistemology are long overdue.

References

Brown, G. and Atkins, D. (1988), *Effective Teaching in Higher Education*. London: Methuen.

Boud, D. and Walker, D. (1990), 'Making the Most of Experience', *Studies in Continuing Education*, **12** (2), 32–47.

Boud, D., Keogh, R. and Walker, D. (eds) (1985), *Reflection: Turning Experience into Learning*. London: Kogan Page.

Boud, D., Cohen, R. and Walker, D. (eds) (1993), *Using Experience for Learning*. Buckingham: SRHE and Open University Press.

Burgess, H. and Jackson, S. (1990), 'Enquiry and Action Learning: A New Approach to Social Work Education', *Social Work Education*, **9** (3), 3–19.

Butt, R., Raymond, D. and Yamagishi, L. (1988), *Autobiographic Praxis: Studying the Formation of Teachers' Knowledge*. Paper presented at the annual meeting of the American Educational Research Association, Boston, MA.

Carew, R. (1979), 'The Place of Knowledge in Social Work Activity', *British Journal of Social Work*, **9** (3), 349–64.

Chamberlain, E. (1977), 'Charting a Course: Hazards for the Academic', *Contemporary Social Work Education*, **4** (1), 25–36.

Collins, H., (1989), 'Learning through enculturation', in A. Gellatly, D. Rogers and J.

Sloboda (eds), *Cognition and Social Worlds*. Oxford: Oxford University Press.

Corby, B. (1982), 'Theory and Practice in Long Term Social Work – a Case Study of Practice with Social Service Department Clients', *British Journal of Social Work*, **12** (6), 619–38.

Davies, M. (1984), 'Training: What Do We Think of it Now?', *Social Work Today*, **15** (20), 12–17.

Gardiner, D. (1984), 'Social Work Education and the Transfer of Learning – a Comment', *Issues in Social Work Education*, **4**, 455–7.

Gardiner, D. (1989), *The Anatomy of Supervision: Developing Learning and Professional Competence for Social Work Practice*. Milton Keynes: Open University Press.

Gibbs, I. and Cigno, K. (1986), 'Reflections from the Field: The Experience of Former CSS and CQSW Students', *British Journal of Social Work*, **16** (3), 289–309.

Gore, J.M. and Zeichner, K.M. (1990), 'On becoming a reflective teacher', in Grant, C.A. (ed.) *Preparing for Reflective Teaching*. Boston, MA: Allyn and Bacon.

Gould, N. (1989), 'Reflective Learning for Social Work Practice', *Social Work Education*, **8** (2), 9–19.

Gould, N. (1991), 'An Evaluation of Repertory Grid Technique in Social Work Education', *Social Work Education*, **10** (2), 38–49.

Gould, N. (1993), 'Cognitive Change and Learning from Practice: a Longitudinal Study of Social Work Students', *Social Work Education*, **12** (1), 77–87.

Gray, J. and Gardiner, D. (1992), 'The Impact of Learning on the Quality of Teaching and Learning in Social Work Education', *Issues in Social Work Education*, **9** (1 & 2), 74–92.

Hamilton, M. (1981), 'Fieldwork: The Core of "Academic" Social Work', *Contemporary Social Work Education*, **4** (1), 34–45.

Harris, A. and Russ, J. (1994), 'Self Assessment within the Context of Initial Teacher Education: The Evaluation of an Innovative Approach', *Assessment and Evaluation in Higher Education*, **19** (3), 72–91.

Hearn, J. (1982), 'The Problem(s) of Theory and Practice in Social Work and Social Work Education', *Issues in Social Work Education*, **2**, 95–117.

Holly, M.L. (1989), 'Reflective Writing and the Spirit of Enquiry', *Cambridge Journal of Education*, **19** (1), 70–80.

Holly, M.L. and McLoughlin, C.S. (1989), *Perspectives on Teacher Professional Development*. London: Falmer Press.

James, C. and Denley, P. (1992), 'Using Records of Achievement in an Undergraduate Certificate in Education Course', *Evaluation and Research in Education*, 38–47.

Kelly, G.A. (1955), *The Psychology of Personal Constructs*. New York: Norton.

Knowles, J.G. (1991), *Journal use in Preservice Teacher Education: A Personal and Reflexive Response to Comparison and Criticisms*. Paper presented at the Annual Meeting of Teacher Educators, New Orleans, LA.

Kolb, D.A. (1984), *Experiential Learning*. Englewood Cliffs, New Jersey: Prentice Hall.

Marton, F. (1988), *Phenomenography and the Art of Teaching all Things to all Men*. Paper presented the annual meeting of the American Educational Research Association, April.

Marton, F. and Ramsden, P. (1987), 'Learning skills or skill in learning?', in J.T.E. Richardson, M.W. Eysenck and D. Warren Piper (eds) *Student Learning Research in Education and Cognitive Psychology*. Milton Keynes: Open University Press.

Marton, F. and Saljo, R. (1984), 'Approaches to learning', in F. Marton and R. Saljo (eds), *The Experience of Learning*. Edinburgh: Scottish Academic Press.

Mezirow, J. (1985), 'A critical theory of self-directed learning', in S. Brookfield (ed.), *Self-Directed Learning – From Theory to Practice*. San Francisco: Jossey Bass.

Paley, J. (1987), 'Social Work and the Sociology of Knowledge', *British Journal of Social Work*, **17** (2), 169–86.

Pearson, G. (1975), 'The politics of uncertainty: A study of the socialization of the social worker', in H. Jones (ed.) *Towards a New Social Work*. London: RKP.

Pilalis, J. (1986), 'The Integration of Theory and Practice. A Re-examination of a Paradoxical Expectation', *British Journal of Social Work*, **16**, 79–96.

Reason, P. and Rowan, J. (eds) (1981), *Human Inquiry: A Sourcebook of New Paradigm Research*. Chichester: John Wiley and Sons.

Rumelhart D.E. (1980), 'Schemata: the building blocks of cognition', in R.J. Spiro, B.C. Bruce and W.F. Brewer (eds) *Theoretical Issues in Reading Comprehension*. New Jersey: Hilldale.

Saljo, R. (1979), 'Learning in the Learners' Perspective; Some Common Sense Conceptions', *Reports from the Department of Education*, University of Goteborg, No. 76.

Saljo, R. (1988), 'Learning in educational settings. Methods of inquiry', in P. Ramsden (ed.), *Improving Learning New Perspectives*. London: Kogan Page.

Schön, D.A. (1983), *The Reflective Practitioner*. London: Temple Smith.

Schön, D.A. (1987), *Educating the Reflective Practitioner*. New York: Basic Books.

Schutz, A. and Wagner, H.R. (eds) (1970), *On Phenomenology and Social Relations*. Chicago and London: University of Chicago Press.

Shaw, I. and Walton, R. (1978), 'Education for Practice: Former Students' Attitudes to a Social Work Course', *Contemporary Social Work Education*, **2** (1), 15–29.

Sims, R. (1981), *Assessing Competencies in Experiential Learning Theory: A Person Job Congruence Model of Effectiveness in Professional Careers*, Unpublished PhD dissertation, Case Western Reserve University.

Smith, N.J. and Sandford, R. (1980), *A Study of Newly Qualified Social Workers in Australia*, Part 1. Melbourne: Monash University.

Stevenson, O. and Parsloe, P. (1978), *Social Service Teams: The Practitioner's View*. London: HMSO.

Syson, L. and Baginsky, M. (1981), *Learning to Practice*. London: CCETSW.

Thomas, L. and Harri-Augstein, S. (1985), *Self Organised Learning: Foundations of a Conversational Science for Psychology*. London: Routledge and Kegan Paul.

Van Rossum, E.J. and Schenk, S.M. (1984), 'The Relationship Between Learning Conception Study Strategy and Learning Outcome', *British Journal of Educational Psychology*, **54**, 11–45.

5 Teaching social work as a reflective process

Ken Moffatt

Within the field of social work we have been quite successful in developing theoretical frameworks for teaching practice. Formal theoretical models, such as the ecological or systems approach to social work, are useful paradigms which help social work students conceptualize their practice interventions. At the same time, however, students within schools of social work are learning certain dispositions to everyday practice within their field placement settings, voluntary activities and part-time employment. We have been less successful as social work educators in helping students reflect on how they become informed through direct practice experience.

There has been a tendency within the field of social work to organize our thinking in categorical and dichotomous ways. We often talk about the subjective or the objective nature of an intervention as if the one is separate from the other. Similarly, we tend to differentiate the micro- from the macro-level of intervention and associate differing skills with each level of intervention. At the same time, practice methods are often defined according to whether they reflect the exercise of social control, social change or social mediation.

Although these conceptualizations are useful in helping students understand how to situate themselves within the profession they may be creating a constraint on how they think about the nature of social work practice. In order to understand practice we need to move away from dichotomies such as the micro and the macro (Vayda and Bogo 1991), and the subjective and the objective (Rossiter 1993; Wacquant 1992). Although categorical thinking is useful for formal modes of thinking and theoretical development it may obfuscate an authentic knowledge of practice.

In this chapter I explain how I taught social work practice as a reflective process to a class of Canadian social work students. The students were in the fourth and final year of a baccalaureate programme. It is the assumption of this paper that there is much for the educator and the student to learn from investigating how the social work student comes to an understanding of a person's well-being through practice. Recent developments in the literature, both within and outside the profession of social work, allow us to reframe the way that social work practice is taught. Drawing predominantly from three major schools of thought, feminist caring and 'growth in connection' literature, the social work literature focused on interpretive methods and the work of French sociologist Pierre Bourdieu (1980), I define pedagogical principles and elaborate teaching methods for teaching social work practice as a reflective process.

Social work within bureaucracy

Many social work students complain that the structures of the organizations in which they work restrict their ability to help clients in a meaningful way. By the time the social work students have reached fourth year within a baccalaureate programme most of them have worked in a field placement within a bureaucratic setting. Students know the tension between their expectations of practice in placement settings and the structural constraints of the agencies in which they are placed. The tension, that students know so well, is a useful starting point for teaching practice. Students begin to realize how the reality of practice circumstances can result in the distortion of their good intentions as a practitioner. By helping students to understand their environmental or social constraints an educator can encourage them to consider new possibilities for practice.

In the classroom I conceptualized the bureaucratic social welfare institution as a social field. According to Bourdieu, a social field is based on a patterned configuration of relationships. Social workers within agencies struggle either to preserve or to change the boundaries and rules of the field (the agency), depending upon their position within it. The students soon realize that they are not simply involved in placement within a stagnant institution but that they are involved in struggles within a social field. Their marginalized position as students within the agency provides a good vantage point from which to understand the regulative principles and values that are promoted within the organization (Wacquant 1992).

The bureaucracy is a useful social context to explore with students since it reflects some of the broader cultural biases within the North American context. The social welfare bureaucracy is structured to reflect an understanding of change as linear in nature. In North America the linear assumption of growth and change has been coupled with a type of optimism that assumes change is progressive. It is assumed that any form of change in a controlled intervention brings us to an improved state of being (Grant 1969; Lasch 1991).

Theory defining clinical practice and human development has also reflected Anglo-North American cultural assumptions such as the values of individualism, competition and the personal will to action. Contemporary models of human development have been critiqued for their cultural bias which assumes that the preferred stage of development is autonomy or the individuated self (Jordan 1991b). Furthermore, models of human development have been challenged for the information that they leave out, such as a person's experience due to race, class, gender or sexual orientation (Rossiter 1993).

At the same time, traditional cultural interactions of social groups are replaced by rationalized, simplified relations within corporate bureaucracies. The milieu for the helping professions is often characterized by a concern for efficiency and a preoccupation with method. Within many professional social work settings the concerns of the person requiring help are redefined as technical problems (Ellul 1980). The social work student risks removing important facets of interaction with the client from his/her purview by focusing upon the technical solution to problems. Elements of human interaction such as history, philosophy, intuition and the emotional interplay between the worker and the person in need are not considered if one takes a purely technical approach to social work (Goldstein 1991; Saleebey 1991).

Human affairs are structured according to prescriptive technology within the social welfare bureaucracy. Prescriptive technology entails specialization by process. Social workers contribute to the work process by taking on specialized tasks. Social work functions are broken down into identifiable steps. Each step within the process is completed by a worker so that the worker has no control over the total creative process. In this manner technology is not only the application of scientific knowledge but also an agent for ordering relations between people (Franklin 1990).

The relationship between the social work student and the person in need becomes conceptualized in a manner which serves the purposes of the bureaucracy and the technical point of view as much as the needs of the client. For example, the worker is often encouraged to develop a set of objectives leading towards predetermined goals for the client. The implicit understanding of the interview process is that the social worker aids the client to progress to an improved state. The social worker is expected to help the client progress from worse to better or from chaos to order. Of course, one intervenes with the hopes of improvement in the well-being of the client but increasingly the suggestion that the social worker/client relationship can be defined in terms of linear development which is progressive in nature has been brought into question (Jordan 1991b; Kondrat 1992; Renaud 1990).

Congruent with the conceptualization of the growth of the human as a linear and progressive process is the desire to break the process into parts.

When analysing a problem, for example, the social worker is encouraged to define components of a problem and then partialize the problem (Wetzel 1986). Miller (1991) uses Erickson's stages of human development as an example of how we tend to define manageable components in an ongoing process. In Erickson's model the person goes through stages of development moving only to the next stage of development when a struggle has been mastered.

The process which has been broken down and then reconstructed as a series of incremental steps towards a predetermined goal is regulated by the social worker. In fact, Foucault (1979) argues that interaction which is based on the assumption that the beneficiary of the relationship will progress or evolve to a stable endpoint is a form of disciplinary action. The social worker exercises power over the client when he or she assumes evolutionary progress on the macro level and breaks down the interaction into a series of events that unfold in a linear manner on the micro level.

The technical, bureaucratic approach to human problems necessarily requires a power imbalance between the client and the worker. If the practice of social workers is defined solely as a technical exercise then practice becomes an arena in which the ideas of the practitioner are worked out on the client in order to develop improved techniques or products (Kondrat 1992).

The interplay of cultural biases, the entrenchment of social work within bureaucratic organizations and the power relationship that social workers have with marginalized groups creates a special concern for social workers. The worker with unshaken confidence in technique and the regulations of bureaucracy may base her or his intervention upon a distorted understanding of human nature. In fact, the technocratic intervention endeavours to reduce social relations to the simple expression of technique and accordingly denies the possibility of a person's social context (Renaud 1990). At the same time, the desire to reach a technical solution to personal and social problems requires the control of a wide variety of variables which may be relevant to an effective intervention (Saleebey 1991).

If the social work student investigates practice reflexively he or she can experience a sense of agency even within the most constraining environment. Even though social welfare bureaucracies can be a frustrating mix of rules and regulations there exists within these settings a structure of possibilities for practice. Playing with the rules, often for the benefit of clients, is as much a part of social work practice as the formalized rules of the agency themselves (Bourdieu and Wacquant 1992).

The social work student draws upon transferable dispositions or 'habitus' in order to achieve tasks related to the client's well-being. These dispositions integrate past experience and are based on perceptions, actions and appreciations (Wacquant 1992). By defining social work practice as habitus it is possible for students to investigate the biases within their personal approach to practice and to understand how those biases are partially formed through social constraints. They can also begin to distinguish those elements of practice which are creative from those which are oppressive in nature.

A paradigm for reflective practice

Technical formal rationality may be well-suited to the management tasks of social work which include planning, coordinating and controlling functions (Franklin 1990), however it is problematic for other tasks of social work such as social mediation or social change. It is necessary, therefore, to reconsider the social work process and become self-conscious about our roles as social workers (Bourdieu and Wacquant 1992).

A fundamental assumption of this paradigm for teaching reflective practice is that people grow in connectedness with others through relationship (Davis 1985). At the same time, it is assumed that knowledge is constituted through interpersonal connection rather than being developed in isolation (Dore 1994). This is particularly important since the majority of the social work students I teach are female. It has been argued that women are socialized to define their self through their interaction with others and their caring function within relationships (Baines 1991; Davis 1985; Gilligan 1982). Miller (1991) contends that a woman's sense of worth is defined through her caring role within relationships.

By assuming that caring relationships are highly valued by social work students, I was challenged to teach in a way that validated knowledge created from the subjective experience inherent in human interaction (Davis 1985). Social work students can be taught practice so that they become aware of the information that is received while in a relationship with a client. This exercise not only helps the social work student better to understand her role but it validates her experience in field placement.

The social work interview, therefore, is conceptualized as an inquiry in which the worker, as well as the client, learn in relationship. The social work student in placement and the client become aware of themselves through interaction with each other during the interview process (Orcutt 1990). This understanding of the interaction between the client and the worker requires that the worker be prepared to reflect upon the effect of her presence within the interaction.

It seems that in order to counter the tendency towards technique and the prescriptive approach to social work the social work student needs to begin the investigation of practice in the lived experience of the individual and the interaction between the worker and the client. The social work student can be helped to understand a human's condition and how the person creates meaning both at a personal and a collective level. As the student becomes sensitive to the tacit knowledge which draws from both subjective and objective sources he or she and the client have begun to create a new possibility (Dore 1994; Saleebey 1991).

The process of human growth can be represented as complicated and ongoing in the classroom. When development at either the individual or the social level is conceptualized as dynamic it is not constrained by a mechanistic viewpoint which insists upon orderly, linear progression (Weick 1987). In a person's life there are high moments and there are low moments; there is chaos and there is order. One may move to an improved circumstance socially or psychologically but at other times one may regress. The social worker does not restrict the possibility of growth to a culturally delineated model based upon autonomy and self-reliance or one that is solely defined by the regulations of bureaucracy.

The case for teaching and practising social work in a reflexive manner has been made by a number of social work authors (Goldstein 1991; Papell and Skolnik 1992; Vayda and Bogo 1991). In order to teach reflective practice the social work interview can be understood to involve a multitude of changes of direction; at times there appears to be little order in interaction. In fact, it is assumed that confusion for the social work student can be good since it means that new information has been received which allows for the possibility of a new interpretation of the client's reality (Schön 1983).

The notion of reflection-in-action suggests that the creative practitioner sets a particular frame to solve a problem. At the same time, he or she is open to the discovery of phenomena and information which may be incongruent with the initial frame. The surprising consequences which occur when one imposes a particular frame on practice can be used to help reframe the question or create new ends to the practice (Schön 1983).

In order to be sensitive to the complicated nature of process and to draw students away from a technical understanding of the interview it is assumed that there are significant moments within the interview that can be determined and discussed. Empathy, for example, is valued and is assumed to be important in understanding a human's needs. Empathic moments occur when the social work student recognizes an essential human sameness with the client. Rather than viewing empathy as a secondary and non-essential emotional response based in confusion it is considered a resource to the social work student (Jordan 1991a).

Furthermore, intuition is respected as a way of knowing. Wetzel (1986) argues that feminist social work practitioners have a dynamic trust in the uniqueness of the individual. This trust is manifest in a willingness to accept non-objective or qualitative ways of knowing. The social worker respects subjective experience, intuition and personal knowledge.

Schön (1983), at the same time, reminds us that intuition is a part of the everyday practice of professionals. He points out that professionals often act in a spontaneous manner that does not rely on a prior intellectual operation. The social work student can learn to be confident in his/her intuitive reaction to circumstances within the interview process. At the same time, intuition is one of those 'moments of knowing' which should be open to inquiry to ensure that it is used in a responsible manner.

Moments of confusion and emotion are not thought to limit the social work student's effectiveness. Those moments are reconceptualized as moments of opportunity for the student since they provide an invitation for the social work student to reconsider his/her intervention. It is unrealistic to assume that confusion can be avoided within human interaction. To ignore those moments may be to ignore some of the most valuable information offered to the worker since that information invites reflection.

The reflective stance not only allows students to think about the information that they receive during the social work interview but also invites them to consider their personal influence on the interaction. Since it is assumed that growth happens in a relationship it is useful to take a stance that considers the intervention of the social worker who so often acts as an objectifier of another person's experience (Bourdieu and Wacquant 1992). Critical reflexivity not only allows for the social work student to become aware of that which they know through practice but also brings forward this knowledge in a manner that it can be considered for inquiry and critique (Kondrat 1992).

The social work student can consider how his/her roles as bureaucrat and as professional social worker influence the way in which the client tells his/her story. The desire of social workers to organize themselves as a professional group which aspires to objectivity and rigour has an influence on the interpersonal interaction with the client. In social work schools students are taught the logic of the detached professional and they bring this logic to their practice. There is a risk that the social work student will impose his/her knowledge as a type of master narrative which subjugates the story of the client and undervalues the knowledge from which the client draws to understand his/her circumstances (Foucault and Gordon 1980; Hartman 1992; Rossiter 1993).

Through reflection in practice the social work students investigate the presuppositions of social workers as well as define those moments when their particular intervention has taken on the quality of imposition of knowledge upon the client. In this manner one is not simply reflecting upon the actions of the individual social work student in the classroom but also on the constitution of practice within the entire field of social work: the study of the interventions of social work students is a study of both the universal and the particular (Bourdieu 1980).

The classroom experience

Registration within the class was capped at twenty-five students so that the students could be divided into two separate smaller groups for role plays. Twenty-three of the students were in the fourth year of the Bachelor of Social Work programme. The students had exposure to at least two field placement settings. Some of the students had extensive experience within the field of social work.

Most of the students in the class were born either outside of Canada or were first-generation Canadians. Many of the students were white and came from a variety of ethnic backgrounds including Portuguese, Italian, Polish, Macedonian, Hungarian and French. Two students were from East Asian backgrounds and one student was Asian from Hong Kong. A female student was a native Canadian. Only three of the students were male. One female student openly identified herself as a lesbian and one of the male students openly identified himself as a gay male.

The course content was organized in three sections. In the first section the constraints of the technical culture within the bureaucracy were defined for the class through lecture and discussion. The second section of the course involved the videotape of role plays between students. There were two primary methods used in order to help students be reflective with respect to the videotaped role plays. Students were expected to keep written journals as well as engage in classroom discussion of the role play during a replay of the recorded interaction. The use of role plays and process recording as teaching methods are suitable to the inductive nature of learning practice through reflection (Papell and Skolnik 1992). Finally, my lectures towards the end of term became a constant process of reflection and clarification.

I explained to the students that the classroom experience was to be conceptualized as the ongoing accomplishment of the social creation of knowledge to which they were party. The classroom became an experimental space in which the students and myself explored how social reality is created through a variety of decisions, actions and 'cognitions of consciousness'. We explored together that which was immediate and familiar to the social work student in the social work process (Wacquant 1992).

It was counterproductive to talk in definitive terms about what was right or wrong in practice because of the purpose of the class. I was not the sole source of objective truth, rather the students and I explored together the nature of the interview process. There was a conscious effort to avoid dualisms which would be created by having myself the sole repository of correct knowledge (Dore 1994).

In fact, the students were reminded that the task was indeed something quite different from learning the correct content for the social work interview. We were exploring the nature of human process together. On the one hand, we were exploring how subjectivity, mundane knowledge and practical competence at the interpersonal level contribute to the nature of our socially approved systems of understanding (Wacquant 1992). On the other hand, we were watching how the social worker's disposition to practise influenced the interaction between the client and the worker.

The students constructed the case scenarios for the role plays; the role plays were derived from real events within the students' placement. Typical scenarios described by the students dealt with matters such as cross-cultural sensitivity and gender relations. Typical settings in which the students were placed included hospitals, child welfare agencies, women's shelters and schools.

The descriptions of the scenarios were used simply to outline the basics of the interaction; the role play within the classroom was allowed to take on a life of its own. Since students were asked to focus upon tacit knowledge that was based in practice they were reminded that we were learning about what was happening in the interaction within the classroom. Students were discouraged from thinking that they could directly replicate the classroom experience in placement at a later date. The lesson was to inform practice in the field rather than to determine the future interactions of the students with their clients.

Role plays were videotaped. The artificial nature of the role play and the further mediation of the relationship through the video screen was a limiting factor in the experience. Students were reminded that we could not watch genuine growth through relationship but that we could receive adequate information to develop a reinterpretation of our understanding of practice.

The preoccupation with being democratic and allowing every student a chance to be videotaped was problematic since it was confusing the focus of the class. This was not a lesson, in the strictest sense, in the technique and content of the social work interview. The role plays were meant to give us information so that we could consider process and the changing position of the social worker. It was necessary, therefore, to change the structure of the class so that every student was not required to be in a role play. If an interview within the class seemed to be dynamic and engaged we would stick with that interview and use it for investigation.

The videotaped role plays were played back within the classroom so we could observe the interaction. The students were asked to make certain observations that were related to practice as a reflective process. Our first exercise, using the taped interview, was simple; we tracked changes of direction during the interview process. The students were asked to indicate when they were surprised by new information and to indicate when they saw a change of direction in the interview. They were then asked to consider why the change occurred and what information might have contributed to the change. Finally, the students were invited to consider when the person who was seeking assistance instigated the change in direction.

Students were then asked to consider how information was used in order to create a hunch about the nature of the client's personal and social circumstances. The information that a social work student draws upon is varied in nature ranging from emotional response to body language and from cognitive content to silence. We watched for the rich source of information and how that information was formulated into a hunch by the social work student.

We tracked how information became available to the worker within the role play and described the nature of the information. Students were then invited to consider how they had combined a variety of pieces of information, such as body language, tone, asides, to create a hunch. They increasingly became aware of how they combined disparate pieces of information in a complex skill of problem solving while still being present to the other person.

In fact, we considered how the student used information in the context of openness to the total experience of the other person and allowed for the other person to influence the interaction (Franklin 1990; Weick 1987). It was necessary to emphasize the synthesis of the information which was received during the role play rather than allow for the compartmentalization of that information (Wetzel 1986).

The class was structured so that social work practice was taught in a generative style rather than a normative style. The social work interview was represented as a process which invited numerous generative possibilities (Saleebey 1993). When a moment was defined as significant, either by myself or a student, the video replay was stopped and the students were asked to give reasonable hunches as to what they interpreted to be happening. Often there were as many as five or six interpretations and each of these explanations was reasonable. We moved in this way from the rational and controlled environment to one in which there was an openness to interpretation. After the hunches were shared we watched what actually happened between the client and the social work student in the role play. We were able to consider the goodness of fit for our alternative interpretations of the interaction.

The students became aware of multiple interpretations. In light of these many interpretations it was easier for the students to understand that the worker can switch positions within an interview when the hunch they are acting on has shifted from a useful reference point to an imposition on the client. The students became aware of the need to progress in a tentative manner so that their interventions were open to revision based upon subsequent knowledge received during the interactions (Vayda and Bogo 1991).

One of the strengths of reflective practice is that it allows the social work student to be open to the subjective element of the experience and to use it as a resource. Subjectivity was not considered a secondary reaction that needed to be contained. In fact, Papell and Skolnik (1992) argue that one of the strengths of social work practice is the openness to the affective aspects of process.

The social work student was encouraged to talk about moments when he or she experienced an empathic response. The social work student is likely to be functioning with both cognitive and emotional awareness elevated during the empathic experience (Jordan 1991b). Students were asked to consider intuitive or gut reactions to what was taking place within the role play. Finally, they were asked to think about moments which they would subjectively define as quality moments. They were also encouraged to express what they were thinking about at that time so they became aware that affective functioning does not preclude cognitive functioning.

Teaching the concepts of empathy, intuition and quality moments allows the students to imbue the objective with the subjective. They become aware that the reasonableness of their interpretations could be heightened by their emotional response, particularly when it is expressed in the context of caring. Affective connection with the client was therefore not a distortion of the social work role rather it was a part of growth through relationship.

The students were encouraged to draw from the richness of the experience of human interaction. They were reminded that their hunches about another person's life were not definitive answers. In fairness and respect to the client they need to proceed in a tentative manner. The social work student learned to be prepared to allow for a change of direction in the interview, all the while reflecting on the relation between herself or himself and the client. It was important that I model this type of reflective practice as the instructor.

Rossiter (1993) reminds us that the academic setting is a bureaucracy. We must be careful, therefore, to avoid a relationship with the students which promotes domination by the lecturer and rigidity in thought. The classroom can be a place where students are allowed to experience themselves as agents of change. One of the primary means of achieving this learning is through the development of relations of mutuality between the instructor and the student within the class.

The emancipatory classroom environment can be achieved if the authority within the classroom is shared with the student rather than located solely with the professor (Dore 1994; Rossiter 1993). I told the students that I expected to achieve greater clarity through relationship with them. The observation of role plays proceeded as if the student and I were exploring the nature of interaction together. Part of the learning for the students occurred when I admitted to being confused or perplexed. At those moments I asked the class to reconsider what we had observed so that we could come to some clarification together. In this way, the students learned that my understanding of social work practice was tentative at times and therefore open to the critical awareness of the students (Rossiter 1993).

The teaching process was a model of reflective practice. At the beginning of the course I cautioned students to expect that the course outline was no more than a framework within which to work. They were told in the first class that the course was a reflective inquiry therefore they should expect many changes of direction and surprising results in their learning. For example, after one particularly intense role play about an abusive relationship I did not interrupt a long silence but rather allowed for an affective response from the class. Rather than try cognitively to interpret the affect of the class I simply pointed out our surprising reaction to the role play.

Lectures were always arranged so that students could interrupt. I erred on the side of letting discussion within class be wide-ranging to allow for serendipitous learning. At times, I put my lecture material away in favour of the classroom discussion. If students were engaged in a dynamic discussion I consciously situated myself so that I could reflect on the discussion rather than control it. At the end of each class I asked generalized questions of the students such as: is there anything else that you have learnt today?

Towards the end of the term I repeated points I had made earlier in the term. In effect, I talked about the same idea from a variety of perspectives. At the end of the course students were asked to contribute to the construction of the concepts we had developed in class. In the second to last class, using the board, we constructed a model for reflective practice together. The last class of the term was set aside for the students to reflect on their learning. I encouraged them to talk about those ideas which they continued to find confusing as well as those ideas which had become concrete for them.

The relationship between myself and the students was attended to so that roles changed as students became more confident through their learning. I shared with the students both affective and intellectual responses to involvement within the classroom (Dore 1993). Acknowledgement was given when a student helped me to consider the role plays or lecture material in a new light. When I decided to change the content or direction of the course based on information I received from the students I made the students conscious of my decision and the information from which it was derived.

Discussion

Both written and oral student evaluations were clearly in favour of learning social work practice as a reflective process. In fact, some of the mature students began to make the case for making reflective practice central to the social work curriculum. If there was a consensus amongst students over the strength of the model it was that learning a reflexive approach to practice allowed them to draw from knowledge that they had thought of as 'soft knowledge' in the past. They felt that certain aspects of their personal practice that had gone unnoticed before were validated in the class.

A student from a First Nations community felt that the model of reflective practice was well-suited to working with native populations. She argued that the history of native populations in Canada is fraught with examples of the infringement upon their cultural integrity by federal social welfare bureaucracies. In fact, she argued within her paper for the class that the model of the reflective social work practitioner was congruent with cultural concepts within her native community.

In an emotional statement in class the gay male student said that he valued the reflective approach because he could take information from an interaction, tuck it away and draw from it later on. He went on to say that its real strength was that it allowed him to use both his head and his heart in practice.

A female student described to me an experience that was akin to a paradigm shift. Since taking this course she understood her experience as a student in other classes and in field settings in a new way. She explained that the lessons from this course were applicable beyond social work practice. For example, the paradigm shift helped her better to understand the content of an optional course on postmodernist literature. In her literature class she was learning about the reflexive approach to literature and the importance of questioning the certitude of the author's point of view.

The most interesting comment, however, came from a student who said she had begun to feel crazy in her field placement setting. After taking this class she realized she was 'not crazy at all but that she was a woman'.

Teaching which focuses on reflection in practice provides the students with a sense of agency; they come to see themselves as actors who can influence relationships even in the most constraining of social welfare bureaucracies. The students become aware of their influence even in the simplest of social work interviews. It seems to me that the most mundane of social work tasks become replete with meaning since the students are reminded that they are engaged in human communication and the construction of meaning. Students grow to understand that they are constructing social realities that make sense to them and the person in need. Some agreement can be reached between the social work student and the client with respect to that which is relevant and indeed how to typify the experience to make sense of the world.

The strength of teaching reflective practice which is based in relationship is that it need not oversimplify the process of human interaction. A reflective practitioner deals with both the cognitive and the emotional understanding of the client, valuing both as informative to the process. Interactions in class which seemed quite simple at first developed a complexity and fullness that was astonishing upon reflection.

At the same time, the disposition of social work students to practice is brought to light. Methods which seem to be self-evident or based in common-sense in the social work interview are brought forward for the critical purview of the students. Also, practice behaviours which are often thought of as informal and tangential to social work practice are given a legitimacy within the classroom.

A surprising result of allowing for reflection in class was that the students began to reflect not only on the nature of the social work interview but also upon the nature of social work as a discipline in the North American context. In one of my most rewarding moments in the class I listened as students discussed social work issues switching between the nature of the micro interaction, such as the respectful stance to take with a client, and macro social work concerns such as the nature of professional knowledge. They also spoke about practice as a process which could be both reasonable and subjective at once. With this shift from categorical and dichotomous thinking the students were open to reconsidering the assumptions and presuppositions that they brought to the practice setting as social work students. In class, they had become engaged participants reflecting on the nature of process through their interaction with each other.

References

Baines, C. (1991), 'The professions and an ethic of care,' in C. Baines, P. Evans and S. Neysmith (eds), *Women's Caring, Feminist Perspectives on Social Welfare*. Toronto: McClelland and Stewart Inc.

Bourdieu, P. (1980), *The Logic of Practice*. Stanford: Stanford University Press.

Bourdieu, P. and Wacquant, L. (1992), 'The purpose of reflexive sociology', in P. Bourdieu and L. Wacquant (eds), *An Invitation to Reflexive Sociology*. Chicago: University of Chicago Press.

Davis, L. (1985), 'Female and Male Voices in Social Work', *Social Work*, March–April, 106–13.

Dore, M. (1993), 'The Practice–Teaching Parallel in Educating the Micropractitioner', *Journal of Social Work Education*, 29 (2), 181–90.

Dore, M. (1994), 'Feminist Pedagogy and the Teaching of Social Work Practice', *Journal of Social Work Education*, 30 (1), 97–105.

Ellul, J. (1980), *The Technological System*. New York: Continuum Publishing Corp.

Foucault, M. (1979), *Discipline and Punish*. New York: Vintage Books.

Foucault, M. and Gordon, C. (eds), (1980), *Power/Knowledge: Selected Interviews and Other Writings, 1972–1977*. New York: Pantheon Books.

Franklin, U. (1990), *The Real World of Technology*. Toronto: C.B.C. Enterprises.

Gilligan, C. (1982), *In a Different Voice, Psychological Theory and Women's Development*. Cambridge: Harvard University Press.

Goldstein, H. (1991), 'Qualitative Research and Social Work Practice: Partners in Discovery', *Journal of Sociology and Social Welfare*, XVIII (4), 101–17.

Grant, G. (1969), *Technology and Empire, Perspectives on North America*. Toronto: House of Anansi.

Hartman, A. (1992), 'In Search of Subjugated Knowledge', *Social Work*, **37** (6), 483–4.

Jordan, J. (1991a), 'Empathy and self boundaries', in J. Jordan, A. Kaplan, J. Miller, I. Stiver and J. Surrey (eds), *Women's Growth in Connection*. New York: The Guilford Press.

Jordan, J. (1991b), 'Empathy, mutuality and therapeutic change', in J. Jordan, A. Kaplan, J. Miller, I. Stiver and J. Surrey (eds), *Women's Growth in Connection*. New York: The Guilford Press.

Kondrat, M. (1992), 'Reclaiming the Practical: Formal and Substantive Rationality in Social Work Practice', *Social Service Review*, **66** (2), 237–55.

Lasch, C. (1991), *The True and Only Heaven: Progress and Its Critics*. New York: W.W. Norton & Co.

Miller, J. (1991), 'The development of women's sense of self', in J. Jordan, A. Kaplan, J. Miller, I. Stiver and J. Surrey (eds), *Women's Growth in Connection*. New York: The Guilford Press.

Orcutt, B. (1990), *Science and Inquiry in Social Work Practice*. New York: Columbia University Press.

Papell, C. and Skolnik, L. (1992), 'The Reflective Practitioner: A Contemporary Paradigm's Relevance for Social Work Education', *Journal of Social Work Education*, **28** (1), 18–26.

Renaud, G. (1990), 'Travail Social, Crise de la Modernité et Post-Modernité', *Revue Canadienne de Social Service*, **7** (1), 27–48.

Rossiter, A. (1993), 'Teaching from a Critical Perspective, Towards Empowerment in Social Work Education', *Canadian Social Work Review*, **10** (1), 76–90.

Saleebey, D. (1991), 'Technological Fix: Altering the Consciousness of the Social Work Profession', *Journal of Sociology and Social Welfare*, **XVIII** (4), 51–67.

Saleebey, D. (1993), 'Theory and the Generation and Subversion of Knowledge', *Journal of Sociology and Social Welfare*, **XX** (1), 5–25.

Schön, D. (1983), *The Reflective Practitioner, How Professionals Think in Action*. New York: Basic Books.

Vayda, E. and Bogo, M. (1991), 'A Teaching Model to Unite Classroom and Field', *Journal of Social Work Education*, **27** (3), 271–8.

Wacquant, L. (1992), 'The structure and logic of Bourdieu's sociology', in P. Bourdieu and L. Wacquant (eds), *An Invitation to Reflexive Sociology*. Chicago: University of Chicago Press.

Weick, A. (1987), 'Beyond Empiricism: Toward a Holistic Conception of Social Work', *Social Thought*, **XII** (4), 36–46.

Wetzel, J. (1986), 'A Feminist World View Conceptual Framework', *Social Casework: The Journal of Contemporary Social Work*, March, 166–73.

6 Using imagery in reflective learning

Nick Gould

Introduction

Social work has been bedevilled in the past by a literature which consists of cookery book-like recipes for good practice. Practice is characterized as the stepwise application of a series of procedures which are deduced from a body of empirical or theoretical knowledge. The contexts within which these rule-governed procedures will be appropriately followed are described within the text, and their recognition assumed to be unproblematic to the practitioner. Similarly, any professional or organizational failures within social work are typically addressed by the development of new procedures or rules to be applied whenever similar circumstances recur.

This persistent faith in the adequacy of an unproblematic rational–deductive view of knowledge and the formulations of rules to promote effective social work are, however, difficult to sustain in the light of wider contemporary social theory. As Wittgenstein showed, and his arguments have been further amplified by a series of social scientists such as Winch (1958), Bloor (1983) and Collins (1985), rules (or lists of injunctions for good practice) cannot logically contain the rules for their own application. The mechanistic application of rules or procedures implicitly depends upon reference to further rules for guidance and these in turn require further rules for their usage, in a potentially infinite regress. How we apply a rule (and how a social worker applies theory to practice) will always be mediated by judgements utilizing forms of knowledge and mental processes which cannot be captured by rational–deductive logic. Indeed, what saves us from social and professional paralysis, from sliding into an infinite regress every time we make a decision or resolve to perform an act, is that we fall back upon judgements which derive from locations outside of formal theory ('Explanations come to an end somewhere' (Wittgenstein 1958; 1)).

Lakoff (1987), summarizing the contemporary field of cognitive science, which incorporates post-Wittgensteinian ideas from a range of disciplines including psychology, sociology, computer science, linguistics and anthropology, identifies the following characteristics of human reason:

- Thought is *embodied*, that is our core conceptual systems grow out of experience of a physical and social nature.
- Thought is *imaginative*, and it is through metaphor, metonymy and mental imagery that we transcend the limitations of direct experience to enable abstract thought and creativity. However, imaginative thought is still embodied, albeit indirectly in experience.
- Thought has *gestalt properties*. Concepts have a totality which is greater than their constituent parts.
- Thought has an *ecological structure* and the effectiveness of cognitive processing (e.g. learning and memory) is dependent upon the overall structure of the conceptual system.

Reflective learning starts from the position confirmed by Lakoff's first proposition that learning is grounded in experience. Addressing the second proposition, this chapter will suggest that the concept of 'imaginative thought' provides an important – if still contested and evolving – approach to understanding the epistemology of practice. If this is so then a key role for social work educators is to help student practitioners to articulate and review the images that underpin their assumptive world. The premise which underlies this argument is that linguistic and pictorial images are media through which our individual and collective senses of reality are constructed. Conversely, language and images are active agents in constructing our experience of ourselves and others. The reasons for proposing the centrality of mental manipulation of images as being a core process in reflective learning and reflective practice derive from a network of contributing arguments which are related, in no order of priority, to theories of creativity, epistemology, social constructivism and values:

Creativity

The recognition of a connection between imagery and creativity has a very long genesis (DanielsMcGhee and Davis 1994). Plato suggested that imagery had a function in the structuring of memory, whilst Aristotle considered imagery to be the source of thought context, and Renaissance philosophers wrote about the use of imagery as an active aid to memory. There is a considerable amount of autobiographical material which indicates that individuals who would be conventionally regarded as creative report that the manipulation of mental imagery has been part of the process of creation (DanielsMcGhee and Davis 1994). Also, cognitive research into problem solving shows the importance of the mental generation of images which can be manipulated to test hypothetical solutions (Kosslyn 1983). Visualization and imaging have also been shown experimentally to be related to performance improvement in various sports (Cratty 1984) with images apparently providing a mental model for guiding, monitoring and fine tuning of complex motor skills (Calderhead and Robson 1991).

The creativity-imagery research also provides interesting, albeit indirect evidence, confirming aspects of the reflective learning cycle. This suggests that creative problem solving often combines sequences of engagement with a problem, subsequent intensive mental work involving the manipulation of images to find a solution, and then a period of attention to other matters, with new insights or solutions emerging apparently spontaneously from 'unconscious cerebration'. This emergence of creativity does not occur without the previous investment of purposeful engagement with the problem. Although deriving from a different field of academic inquiry, the creativity literature confirms the significance of reflection-on-action as a necessary stage to the generation of solutions to problems.

Epistemology

Imagery and metaphor (word-based images) are not simply the ornament or illustration of an underlying reality, but are themselves constitutive of knowledge. Lakoff and Johnson in *Metaphors We Live By* (1980) show the universality and necessity of categorization of experience through the medium of imagery acting at a meta-level. This is a reflexive process by which human beings actively categorize experience, but also their own subjectivity is constructed through the images and metaphors which are current in their 'forms of life'. Some of the best exemplars of this process come from the history of science showing how the genealogy of knowledge in which ideas which have to be expressed imaginistically to communicate concepts which are counter-intuitive or not directly apprehensible by sensory perception, become established as having their reality and construct our understanding of the world (Faraday's theory of magnetic 'fields' or Rutherford's model of atomic structure as a planetary system would be examples). Conversely, the exploration and deconstruction of images and metaphors involves hypothesizing about the organization of ideas, their inter-relationship and their social embeddedness (Tourangeau 1982).

Social constructivism

A related epistemological argument emerges from those strands of intellectual history in the twentieth century which can be characterized as social constructivism. Symbolic interactionism, for instance, emphasizes interpretation and meaning as the basis of an understanding of human interaction and the construction of social reality (Berger and Luckman 1972). Berger and Luckman draw heavily upon the work of George Mead, via Blumer, construing 'reality' as a mediated and negotiated concept which develops through the assumption of roles and the imagination of the realities occupied by others within social arenas. It is not an accident that the seminal figures within social constructivism such as Mead and Blumer were closely associated with American pragmatists like John Dewey (see Chapter 1 of this volume) and there is a shared recognition of reflection as a central process in human development.

Schema theory

Amongst writers who are currently exploring the contribution of imagery to the study of practitioner knowledge and learning, there is furthermore an incorporation from cognitive science of 'schema theory'. Although this has come to prominence in such highly contemporary fields as artificial intelligence and communication theory, its importance was anticipated by Immanuel Kant, as recognized in the OED definition of schemata: 'In Kant: Any one of certain forms of rules of the "productive imagination" through which the understanding is able to apply its "categories" to the manifold of sense-perception in the process of realising knowledge or experience'. In their seminal elaboration of the concept, Rumelhart and Ortony (1977) call schemata the building blocks of cognition, the frames of reference upon which information processing depends. Unlike the technical–rational paradigm of inductive reasoning referred to above, schema theory asserts that all knowledge is organized into units which contain within them the rules for the application of knowledge. A schema is a data structure for representing generic concepts stored in memory, including underlying objects, situations, events, sequences of events and programmes of action. Schemata are frameworks for personal knowledge, which constitute informal but often unarticulated theories for interpreting the world which have encoded within them prescriptions for action. Very often schemata will exist as images or metaphors which act as frames within which the content and implications for action of a situation will be determined (Ortony 1980).

Values

A central argument in Lakoff and Johnson is that images and metaphors are media which transcend conventional Western oppositions between subjectivity and objectivity, and between fact and value. A criticism of the place of experiential learning within social work education has been that the focus upon introspection and affect has impeded the development of a knowledge base within social work and the critical incorporation of formal knowledge within practice (Sibeon 1991). On the other hand, social work educators have been concerned that the particular emphasis within social work of the inter-personal requires a complex exploration of inter-relations between cognition, subjectivity and the moral domain. A value of an approach to learning which addresses imagery, as conceptualized within schema theory, is that it offers integrated access to all these areas. Later in this chapter an example is given of a student on placement who drew an image of his practitioner self as an emerging android, half man and half robot. Immediately this image has multidimensionality which includes formal theory (organizational theory, the sociology of the professions), affect (feelings of alienation) and values (perhaps conflicts between procedural equity and Kantian values of respect for the individual). In brief, the evolving analytic and empirical studies of imagery and metaphor offer an understanding of knowledge for practice which is *holistic*.

Professional learning and imagery

There is a growing body of research within professional education which illuminates and extends these discussions of imagery. There is converging evidence that the conceptions which learners bring to their education, through which they attempt to make sense out of confusion, and construct their self-identity as professionals, are cognitively represented as 'metaphors, understood as picture-preferences or language embedded pictures' (Bullough and Knowles 1991, p. 123). This is supported by a growing body of empirical work (Connelly and Clandinin 1988; Munby and Russell 1989; Calderhead and Robson 1991, Gould and Harris in press).

Particularly within research into initial teacher education, the notion of image has proved fertile and suggestive, even though it is used in different ways. Clandinin, for instance, has gathered narratives from classroom teachers and identified within these key metaphors (e.g. 'classroom as home' or 'language as the key') which act as meta-concepts for organizing the way in which teachers' thinking about practice is structured: '[Image] is a personal, meta-level, organising concept in personal practical knowledge in that it embodies a person's experience; finds expression in practice; and is the perspective from which new experience is taken' (Clandinin 1986, p. 166).

Clandinin's images are expressed in language, although, as Ong has argued, linguistic images or metaphors seem to be mentally converted and held by the individual as pictorial mental representations (Ong 1982). Other researchers have used the concept of image to describe a 'cinematic' mental representation of a sequence of events – Calderhead and Robson give an example of how a particular lesson runs (Calderhead and Robson 1991). For others, the term 'images' refers to static mental pictures, such as pupils, which are held as memorized snapshots.

As has already been suggested, a view which surfaces at various points in these studies is that images function as 'schemata' through which processes of accommodation and assimilation contribute, through experiential learning, to the formation of professional self-identity.

Why should social work educators be interested in all this? – beginning images of practice

Alma Harris and I have undertaken a research project to compare the imagery informing experiential learning in social work and initial teacher education (Gould and Harris in press). The research was located methodologically within an interpretive paradigm informed by phenomenology and symbolic interactionism; it sought to understand and interpret students' own perceptions of their experience. The rationale for comparing teacher education with social work education was that both make use of periods of supervised practice to prepare students to become professionally competent in indeterminate areas of practice.

Through semi-structured dialogue with students, narratives were produced which related their images of practice and themselves as beginning practitioners to their personal biographies. In all, thirty teaching students and twenty social work students were interviewed prior to the first of two assessed professional placements about their perceptions, views and understandings of their chosen profession. They were asked to recall experiences which had directly influenced their decision to enter social work, and the images they currently held of themselves as practitioners.

The beginning imagery of teachers was heavily influenced by the thousands of hours they had spent in 'apprenticeship' as school pupils. This gave them a comprehensive resource of images of teachers who characterized both good and bad practice. The teachers they wished to become were heavily modelled on images of their own teachers they perceived as positive. These images were not explicitly concerned with effective strategies of teaching, but were characterized by personal qualities such as warmth, humour, genuineness and approachability.

By comparison social work students (with some exceptions) had little contact before training with professional practitioners, and furthermore were very conscious of the negative images which are purveyed in the media. When students did have contact with practitioners prior to beginning their courses, this had generally been as volunteers or workers in settings such as day centres or residential homes, and they still presented images of social work which reflected a culture of scepticism. The following quotation from an ex-residential worker conveys the spirit of these images:

> The social workers I have images of are the ones who used to come to the homes I worked in . . . I always used to see them as pains in the arse really. They used to be the people who had all the theory-based things and would come in and say 'This is what I think should be happening' when they don't even know the kids they're talking about.

Harris and I found that the images of practice which social workers had to draw upon were either 'rehearsing for practice' where students, as in the example above, had worked in some unqualified capacity in the social services, or alternatively came from a 'practising skills' category where the student had undertaken a caring role in a personal capacity, often within the family, which was presumed to provide a picture of caring or problem solving which could be transferred into a professional domain. Ours was a small qualitative study, but bears consideration alongside recent American studies which provide substantive evidence that social work students come from backgrounds disproportionately characterized by high levels of family dysfunction and pathology (Russel *et al.*, 1993; Black, Jefferies and Kennedy Hartley 1993). A recent study in the United Kingdom similarly claimed that a disproportionate number of child protection workers had themselves been abused as children (Sone 1995). Even allowing for some methodological caveats in this work, it seems a reasonable deduction from these and our own studies that many social work students bring into the beginning of their education a stock of images which have a negative valency and which may not be the basis for assertive and empowering practice.

Imaginization as praxis

For social work educators this all suggests at least two issues for attention, that the images which students hold of themselves constitute points of access not only to their cognitions which organize and orientate practice, and their value preferences, but also are potentially media of change and development within social work education. Writers on organizational change such as Gareth Morgan see this as constituting a new form of 'praxis', a theoretical framework for action-research but also a reflexive medium by which individuals and groups can empower themselves (Morgan 1993).

Morgan has developed the notion of 'imaginization' as a generic term for the structured processes by which groups and individuals are helped to articulate the images which influence their behaviour, and practice the adaptation of those images as a means of 'reframing' action and finding new approaches to practice. As discussed in Chapter 1, these approaches draw strongly from the pragmatist tradition (which includes writers such as Dewey, Lewin and Argyris) of finding ways of linking theory and practice so that knowledge can be action-based and derived from action in the real world. In addition, Morgan's ideas seem to be closely allied to therapeutic strategies within the Palo Alto school of family therapy, and which in turn, via Bateson, draw on Wittgenstein's theories of language-games as a formative influence (Watzlawick, Weakland and Fisch 1974; Tuson 1985). These ideas centre around the concept of 'reframing', the search to transfer dysfunctional perceptions from an existing conceptual framework to a new more productive image or framework. In turn, this can contribute to the development of capacities for continuous self-organization and self-directed learning (Morgan 1993, p. 17).

Morgan describes his own work as both action-learning and action-research. His methods are also phenomenological and ethnographic – beginning from the inspection of conscious experience. These approaches seek to fuse the development of theory and practice through direct engagement with problem solving rather than through traditional positivist methods of detached study and observation. Indeed, much of Morgan's work takes the form of case studies or – in his own word – 'stories' of collaboration with organizations to address identified strategic problems.

The practice of imaginization is conceptualized as involving five processes which can be generalized to working in learning situations to work with either individuals or groups: first, 'getting inside' – attempting to enter into a situation to understand it as far as possible from the perspective of participants. Secondly, it involves the facilitator in adopting the role of the learner, allowing situations to emerge rather than superimposing external 'expert' formulations. Next, 'mapping the terrain' is necessary by which disparate images are collected and, fourthly, compared to find emergent themes, overlaps and discontinuities. Finally, there is a continuous feedback dialogue with participants to refine and improve the mapping. This process of assisted articulation of images can be taken forward to support the search for new images to frame experience.

Using structured approaches to imaginization in social work education

The following are just two examples of methods I have used in teaching which make planned use of imaginative thought as part of developing students' reflection on action. They are meant to be illustrative and not in any way definitive (Morgan describes a range of additional methods that might be adapted to social work).

Repertory grid technique as a reflective learning method

Repertory grid technique is a well-established method which engages the individual in active imagining of themselves, but can also invite participants to conceptualize themselves as they would like to be. I have argued elsewhere that there are interesting parallels between Schön's epistemology of reflective practice and the earlier ideas of George Kelly who, through his theory of personal construct psychology, characterized his own epistemological position as 'constructive alternativism' (Gould 1989). Donald Schön's formulation of reflective practice is clearly also a contribution to constructivist theories of knowledge with the practitioner behaving as an action-researcher, testing out and modifying hypotheses in the process of intervention. Similarly, Kelly's personal construct psychology views the individual as continuously striving for meaning, but ultimately unable to make contact directly with an interpretation-free reality. Kelly locates his paradigm of learning and development within the metaphor of 'the person as scientist' and Schön within an extended metaphor of 'artistry'. However, for both writers contact with the experienced world is always mediated by those hypotheses or constructs held to be the most reliable, until they are disconfirmed and modified through experience.

Kelly developed repertory grid technique as a method to help elicit those dimensions of meaning which are most significant in the individual's construal of the personal environment. Originally developed by Kelly for use in psychotherapy as a method for mapping the constructs a person used in relation to self and significant relationships, the technique has been diversified enormously in terms of methodology and applications. Similarly, the processes for analysing grid content have been elaborated, now offering a range of possibilities for immediate display of grids on personal computers, with a variety of statistical approaches to their analysis. For those without such resources, there are techniques for manual analysis of grids (Thomas and Harri-Augstein 1985).

Repertory grid technique can be used with individual students or groups as a reflective technique during the period of a practice placement (Gould 1991, 1993). In my own work, students used as elements in the grid, people who they considered to be significant in their learning, including not only professional mentors but also service clients. The grid also contained the elements of 'self', 'the social worker I want to be' and 'the social worker I don't want to be'. Standard repertory grid method was used to elicit the constructs which the elements suggested and the whole grid was rated on a 1 to 5 scale. The grid was then processed on a personal computer using the FOCUS program (Shaw 1980; Thomas and Harri-Augstein 1985) which uses cluster analysis to re-order the grid to show the statistically most significant dimensions between both elements and the constructs. Statistical 'distance' between clusters is also shown as a correlation expressed as a percentage of match. By repeating the grid at intervals during a placement (in this instance on three occasions) a heuristic device is created by which students can respond to apparent changes in their self-image and perception of their learning domain. The completion of each grid was followed by a feedback session which used the FOCUS grid as a starting point for a reflective discussion.

An illustration is provided by the case study of a middle-aged woman who was on the final year of her qualifying social work studies, and who was undertaking a placement with a children's psychiatric facility. She completed and discussed three grids at the beginning, middle and end of her placement, and used the grids as part of the agenda of her supervision meetings with her practice teacher.

Although in all three grids she construed herself as part of a cluster which included professionals, she also placed herself alongside 'Client 1'. In feedback sessions this precipitated long discussions of the student's identification with this client's position as a woman of a similar age. The student reflected on parallels between her own earlier life and development as well as the tasks the client was now facing to assert her own identity and needs. This engendered further discussion of the extent to which this identification arose from similarities of personal biography, and the extent to which they were determined by more structural and political factors relating to the position of women. The constructs most highly matched in the grid, 'stubborn – meek' and 'knows what she wants – indecisive' were seen by the student as critical to herself in her emerging identity as a professional woman, and to her client in resolving family issues. The client's husband is represented in the grid as 'easier client' and his distance from his wife in the grid symbolized the distance which actually existed in the marriage. The student used the grids in supervision to hypothesize her assessment of the family difficulties and possibilities for intervention.

As the placement developed, matching scores between self and practice teacher decreased and increased. This was interpreted by the student in terms of the first half of the placement being characterized by the search for her own professional identity and autonomy, but then later in the placement finding a new relationship with the practice teacher based on mutual respect and an acceptance of difference. Matching scores between 'self' and 'tutor' increased as the placement unfolded which for the student suggested a growing recognition that she and the tutor had similarities of personality, but also that she experienced the tutor as increasingly supportive.

In the follow-up to the project from which this illustration is drawn, sixteen out of eighteen students reported that completing grids and discussing them made them more aware of the assumptions which they brought to their practice, particularly the reductionist and stereotypical labels they could apply to people and their behaviour. Most also found that the most enlightening part of the process was not the completion of the grid but the opportunity for reflection in the feedback discussion.

Using artistic expression in reflective learning

Some students find it helpful to be able to express their imagery graphically by using art materials to make a direct pictorial representation of their view of themselves as practitioners. For many people the prospect of sitting in front of a blank sheet of drawing paper with pencils or brushes to hand invokes discomforting memories of art as a school discipline and the anxiety of our efforts being criticized, assessed and compared. As a method for reflective learning which requires these learning blocks to be overcome, the exercise depends on the establishment of an ethos which draws on a number of the principles which underpin art therapy.

In her writing on art therapy Marian Liebmann gives some useful indicators for educators as to how they might incorporate the use of art materials in class teaching, as well as some of the reasons for seeing them as a valuable resource (Liebmann 1990). First, the practice of making artistic representation is probably universal in childhood, and represents something which everyone can do, provided that the expectations are clearly set that no standards will be applied of technical or cultural 'correctness'. Secondly, pictures are one way of finding a path through problems of articulacy and adopting the right words. This can particularly be the case where the topic is very emotionally charged for the individual; a drawing or painting can side-step some of the difficulties of representing feelings linguistically, but without necessarily foregoing precision.

The process of 'doing art' can itself be helpful in capturing ideas or feelings which were preconscious or in need of clarification. Clearly, drawing or painting are not limited in terms of effect but can also be a vehicle for dealing with ideas and arguments. Provided that there is shared acceptance of a non-judgemental response to the efforts of others, sharing the product can be a powerful medium for stimulating group discussion. In particular, pictorial representation has no fixed interpretation and the exploration of ambiguity and meaning of an individual's art can be a catalyst for group learning.

Finally, no-one is a greater expert on the content of a picture than the person who created it, so the method equalizes participation and is a form of self-directed inquiry. To adopt the pictorial metaphor which itself is a kind of theme within reflective learning, the picture 'frames' experience and provides a context parallel to real life within which alternative possibilities can be rehearsed and redrawn.

There is no prescriptive formula for incorporating art within social work education, but (as with repertory grids) students seem to find it a powerful device when used as a basis for reflection during practice placements. This author has worked with students at the mid-point of the practicum, where the students, using large sheets of art paper and generous amounts of coloured pens, have drawn images of themselves before starting the placement, and their current self-image as practitioners.

For some students the experience is profound and the facilitator needs to be ready to respond to the content of the session seriously and with ample time for discussion and follow-up. Some students present self-images which are quite realistic in content, others produce highly symbolic representations of their situation. A student whose placement required counselling of adolescents who had been abused during childhood drew a picture of a closed box to represent himself before the placement, and a box with an open lid from which a hand and arm were emerging to depict himself at that point in the placement; the experiences of working with abused young people was requiring him to acknowledge difficult experiences within his own childhood. Another student depicted himself as mutating into a robot as the placement progressed, his own metaphorical but direct communication of his anxieties about the impact of front-line statutory work upon the humanistic and radical ideals which brought him to social work.

Some further thoughts

The study of the role and potentiality of imagery in practitioner knowledge continues to evolve. It raises some problems as well as opportunities. An unavoidable question concerns the relationship of formal knowledge, be it abstract theory or empirical research, to reflection on action. There is a real danger of reflective learning becoming a populist bandwagon which legitimates the abandonment of intellectual rigour. We may be critical of the recipe books for practice but there is a corresponding danger of descending into the relativist quagmire. Reflective learning only has value if its effect is to deepen the complexity of practice; rather than rejecting the sphere of the intellect, the reflective paradigm actually requires an engagement with some of the particularly difficult debates within social theory.

For instance, a particular excess of some postmodernist theory (to which reflective learning is increasingly grafted) by virtue of a preoccupation with contingency and diversity has been to deflect attention from the persistence of some forms of social structure, particularly the ways in which patterns of dominance and hierarchy are reproduced (Mouzelis 1995). It is perhaps a useful corrective to reassert the pragmatist contribution to reflective learning which does not deny that there is an external reality which impinges upon peoples' lives, but that there are degrees of adequacy and utility for practice in the ways that reality can be conceptualized.

The rejection of orthodoxy that social work can be characterized as aspiring to a 'scientific' form of rationality moves us towards a conceptualization of practice as a form of craft containing within it a repertoire of skills and judgements (Majone 1989). Within this repertoire a core skill is the critical analysis of the techniques used to produce knowledge and the methods of persuasion and rhetoric employed to advance the truth-value of a particular theoretical claim. The study of imagery and metaphor has direct relevance to this undertaking. For instance, Soyland (1994) has argued in relation to psychology that formal theory is as rhetorical as any other mode of discourse, and the distinctions we make between hard and soft forms of knowledge may be less than often presumed; theoretical writings can be read as 'persuasive texts' which subtly but pervasively use rhetorical devices, particularly metaphor, to assert their claims to truth. Habituation to an idea which is at first transparently metaphorical becomes replaced by the metaphor being eventually taken as a literal truth. One approach then to conceptualizing the contribution of theory to practice is to follow this path of seeing formal texts as a discursive repertoire to be deconstructed by students alongside more personal, experientially derived images of practice.

This approach requires an acceptance that formal knowledge is not ontologically privileged over personal knowledge gained through personal reflection and introspection. Usher and Bryant argue that each make distinct contributions but without one being 'foundational'. Formal theory is directed towards representation and explanation, whereas practitioner knowledge is essentially hermeneutic – about understanding, interpretation and appropriation (Usher and Bryant 1989, p. 189). The relationship between the two is not foundational and rational–deductive, but formal theory presents alternative frames within which practice and intervention can be more or less usefully re-presented and reformulated.

Another issue which requires attention in the consideration of imagery as a component of practice knowledge is that of determinism. Morgan seems to assume that individuals are able to choose their own images and metaphors and to change their behaviour on the basis of these choices. Some researchers in the field of professional education cited in this chapter who agree that images operate as important orientations to practice, worryingly report that images which operate in the early part of a professional career are quite impervious to change. This may reflect a failing on the part of educators to be proactive in facilitating reflective exercises which would encourage shifts in the individual's imagery or frames, but there is obviously a need for more evaluative research of reflective programmes. While it is accepted that some professionals have the capacity for unsupported reflection, many will require some form of facilitation. Similarly while some professionals learn from every experience, others learn from selective experiences which possess certain characteristics or features.

There is a growing body of research into the socialization of social work students and the early development of practitioner knowledge (Gould 1993; Ryan, Fook and Hawkins 1995). This would be complemented by two further forms of research inquiry. In teacher education there has been over the past ten years a significant amount of ethnographical, narrative research with practitioners exploring in detail the images which sustain practice (Clandinin 1986; Bullough and Knowles 1991; Knowles 1993). This has not been replicated in the social work field. Secondly, there is a place for action research on a longitudinal basis which incorporates some of the methods of imaginization to assess whether individuals are able to make use of processes which assist them in reframing their practice on the basis of more productive images.

References

Berger, P. and Luckman, T. (1972), *The Social Construction of Reality*. Harmondsworth: Penguin.

Black, P.N., Jefferies, D. and Kennedy Hartley, E. (1993), 'Personal History of Psychosocial Trauma in the Early Life of Social Work and Business Students', *Journal of Social Work Education*, **29** (2), 171–80.

Bloor, D. (1983), *Wittgenstein – a Social Theory of Knowledge*. New York: Columbia University Press.

Bullough, R. and Knowles, J. (1991), 'Teaching and Nurturing Changing Conceptions of Self as a Teacher in a Case Study of Becoming a Teacher', *Qualitative Studies in Education*, **4** (2), 121–40.

Calderhead, J. and Robson, M. (1991), 'Images of Teaching: Student Teachers' Early Conceptions of Classroom Practice', *Teaching and Teacher Education*, **7** (1), 1–8.

Clandinin, J. (1986), *Classroom Practice: Teacher Images in Action*. London: Falmer Press.

Collins, H.M. (1985), *Changing Order: Replication and Induction in Scientific Practice*. London: Sage.

Connelly, F.M. and Clandinin, J. (1988), *Teachers as Curriculum Planners: Narrative of Experience*. New York: Teachers College Press.

Cratty, B.J. (1984), *Psychological Preparation and Athletic Excellence*. Ithaca, NY: Mouvement Publications.

DanielsMcGhee S. and Davis G.A. (1994), 'The Imagery–Creativity Connection', *Journal of Creative Behaviour*, **28** (3), 151–76.

Gould, N. (1989), 'Reflective Learning for Social Work Practice', *Social Work Education*, **18**, 9–19.

Gould, N. (1991), 'An Evaluation of Repertory Grid Technique in Social Work Education', *Social Work Education*, **10** (2), 38–49.

Gould, N. (1993), 'Cognitive Change and Learning from Practice: A Longitudinal Study of Social Work Students', *Social Work Education*, **12** (1), 77–87.

Gould, N. and Harris, A. (in press), 'Student Imagery of Practice in Social Work and

Teacher Education: a Comparative Research Approach', *British Journal of Social Work*.

Knowles, J. (1993) 'Life-history accounts as mirrors', in J. Calderhead and P. Gates (eds), *Conceptualizing Reflection in Teacher Development*. London: Falmer Press.

Kosslyn, S.M. (1983), *Ghosts in Mind's Machine: Creating and Using Images in the Brain*. New York: W.W. Norton.

Lakoff, G. (1987), *Women, Fire and Dangerous Things*. Chicago: University of Chicago Press.

Lakoff, G. and Johnson, M. (1980), *Metaphors We Live By*, Chicago: University of Chicago Press.

Liebmann, M. (1990), 'Art therapy and other caring professions', in M. Liebmann (ed.), *Art Therapy in Practice*. London: Jessica Kingsley.

Majone, G. (1989), *Evidence, Argument and Persuasion in the Policy Process*. New Haven: Yale University Press.

Morgan, G. (1993), *Imaginization: the Art of Creative Management*. Newbury Park, CA: Sage.

Mouzelis, N. (1995) *Sociological Theory: What Went Wrong?* London: Routledge.

Munby, H. and Russell, T. (1989), 'Metaphor in the study of teachers' professional knowledge', in A. Oberg and G. McCutcheon (eds), *Theory into Practice*, **29** (3), special edition.

Ong, W.J. (1982), *Orality and Literacy; The Technologizing of the World*. London: Methuen.

Ortony, A. (1980), 'Metaphor', in R. Spiro, B. Bruce and W. Brewer (eds), *Theoretical Issues in Reading Comprehension*. Hillsdale: Lawrence Erlbaum Associates.

Rumelhart, D.E. and Ortony, A. (1977), 'Representation of knowledge', in R.C. Anderson, R.J. Spiro and W.E. Montague (eds), *Schooling and the Acquisition of Knowledge*. Hillsdale: Lawrence Erlbaum Associates.

Russel, R., Gill, P., Coyne, A. and Woody, J. (1993), 'Dysfunction in the Family of Origin of MSW and Other Graduate Students', *Journal of Social Work Education*, **29** (1), 121–9.

Ryan, M., Fook, J. and Hawkins, L. (1995), 'From Beginners to Graduate Social Workers: Preliminary Findings of a Longitudinal Australian Study', *British Journal of Social Work*, **25** (1), 17–36.

Shaw, M.L.G. (1980), *On Becoming A Personal Scientist*. London: Academic Press.

Sibeon, R. (1991), *Towards a New Sociology of Social Work*. Aldershot: Avebury.

Sone, K. (1995), 'One in Three', *Community Care*, Issue 1073, 22–28 June, 22–3.

Soyland, A.J. (1994), *Psychology and a Metaphor*. London: Sage.

Thomas, L.F. and Harri-Augstein, S. (1985), *Self-organised Learning: Foundations for a Conversational Science for Psychology*. London: Routledge & Kegan Paul.

Tourangeau, R. (1982), 'Metaphor and cognitive structure', in D.D. Miall (ed.), *Metaphor – Problems and Perspectives*. Brighton: Harvester Press.

Tuson, G. (1985), 'Philosophy and Family Therapy: A Study in Interconnectedness', *Institute of Family Therapy*, **7**, 277–94.

Usher, R. and Bryant, I. (1989), *Adult Education as Theory, Practice and Research: The Captive Triangle*. London: Routledge.

Watzlawick, P., Weakland, J. and Fisch, R. (1974), *Change: Principles of Problem Formulation and Problem Resolution*. New York: W.W. Norton.

Winch, P. (1958), *The Idea of a Social Science and its Relation to Philosophy*. London: Routledge and Kegan Paul.

Wittgenstein, L. (1958), *Private Investigations*, 2nd edn, G.E. Anscombe (trans.). Oxford: Basil Blackwell.

7 Facilitating reflective learning

Imogen Taylor

I am beginning to understand that the paradoxes of my life are related to being a student and teacher of topics that intimately touch my own and other people's lives ... It demands openness to people and absorption of ideas; protection of time and energy, as well as endless commitment to students. It demands the skill of objectivity and observation as well as the involvement, distance as well as intimacy. It demands self-assurance, power and humility. (Freud 1988, p. 135)

Introduction

As a facilitator on a social work education course which is designed to enable students to become self-directed learners, I am constantly confronted with the question of what it means to 'facilitate' the learning of another. This question regularly arises with an immediacy and urgency in a way which it is possible to avoid in the conventional teacher role. As a teacher on a conventional course I can remain in the monological, didactic role of expert, dealing with material at a theoretical level, objectifying both the material and the students, treating the material as if it is private property (Belenky et al 1986). This approach to teaching creates a distance from students which can provide relative immunity from student responses to the effectiveness of teaching. In contrast, in a course which is designed to encourage self-directed learning, in addition to supporting students to learn the knowledge, skills and values required to qualify for practice, my role as facilitator is to help them learn how to learn, an essential skill for lifelong learning. This requires me to be clear about the process of learning and to model that process in my role as a facilitator where both my acts and my words are very visible.

This chapter is about facilitating reflective learning on a social work education course designed to promote self-directed learning. In Chapter 2, David Boud and Susan Knights discuss a number of strategies for building a reflective process in teaching and learning but do not specifically address their implications for the facilitator role. Brookfield (1993) suggests that in our concern to value experience and enable students to contribute to the learning of each other we are in danger of ignoring the educator role and the need to be teacher centred as well as learner centred.

Reflective learning is defined as 'a generic term for those intellectual and affective activities in which individuals engage to explore their experiences in order to lead to new understandings and appreciations' (Boud, Keogh and Walker 1985, p. 19). As discussed in Chapter 1, this is often a non-technical, non-rational process where the emphasis is on the creative and intuitive and the learner becomes confident in responding to the unpredictable and unknown (Schön 1983).

Self-directed learning is defined as having two main components, situational autonomy and epistemological autonomy (Candy 1991). Situational autonomy includes the sense of being in control and self-determining. It refers to the skills necessary for the learner to achieve learning goals and includes the ability to build on existing knowledge, explore questions in depth, be critically aware and monitor learning. These skills are also essential to reflective learning and to learning how to learn. Epistemological autonomy includes acquiring a knowledge base for practice and developing strategies for selecting and obtaining new knowledge. Boud (1988) suggests that self-directed learning also involves learning and working interdependently, a feature of self-directed learning which is central to this chapter where the focus is on the interaction between students and facilitator.

The possibilities for self-directedness in learning are of course governed by the context for learning and the purpose of the learner, both of which in a university social work education course are highly specific. However, in spite of external pressures towards increased prescription about what must be learnt, there continues to be potential within social work education for significant variation in the approaches to teaching and learning.

Becoming a teacher

Brookfield (1993) recommends we use our own experience as learners to provide us with a powerful lens to view our practice as educators. John Cowan (1993) recommends all educators learn about learning by regularly becoming students. Certainly my own experiences as a learner have shaped my orientation as a teacher. An initial key experience was entering the university to earn a professional social work qualification, having competently practised social work as an unqualified worker for seven years. My memory is of real trauma in the first term as I struggled to hold on to some semblance of competence. It was a very disorientating experience and a refusal temporarily to abandon what I knew led to questions by some of my teachers about whether I was really ready to take on the student role. This was an example I now recognize of the situation being problematized and attributed to me, rather than a readiness to examine the educational system which assumed a banking approach to education and insisted on me as blank slate (Freire 1981). For a time the cost of the commitment to social work education certainly seemed greater than the expected rewards (Schön 1987). By the end of the first term I had begun to relocate my sense of competence in the context of connectedness with one or two teachers who validated what I brought to the course.

The second key experience was two years after qualifying as a social worker when I began supervising students and was first challenged to conceptualize the nature of teaching. Much like taking on the role of parent, in working out the role of practice teacher I only had my own experiences as a student to draw on. Fortunately, I had some excellent role models. It was apparent there was more to teaching than telling or modelling; the student was more than an apprentice there to pick up what she could from me. I learnt a great deal from 'my' students about how to contribute to their learning, and in particular came to understand from the practice teacher vantage point the importance of the exchange between teacher and student which had been crucial in my own experience as a student.

The next teaching challenge was when having assumed the mantle of a university teacher in the institution where I qualified, I began to 'teach' social work students communication and interviewing skills. Working with a small group of ten highly competent graduate students for a day a week during their first term meant I was working with students who were very keen to learn not only about interviewing skills but also about the profession. Being in their first term they were swimming about in unfamiliar waters and experiencing 'a loss of competence, control and confidence' and became temporarily dependent on me for 'acquiring understanding, direction and competence' (Schön 1987, p. 94). I recognized the experience the students were having, the challenge became to know how to help them move beyond it and to prepare for practice placements. Schön suggests students in these circumstances must temporarily abandon what they already know and later judge for themselves what was useful. Yet, abandoning what they knew clearly had a deskilling effect which not only seemed wasteful but also very painful.

As my classroom teaching responsibilities expanded, I attempted to transfer my practice knowledge, skills and values to teaching and several practice models were particularly relevant. At the time I was living in Canada and an early significant influence was the humanist approach characterized by the work of Carl Rogers (1982) and congruent with the traditional social work values of genuineness, respect for others and acceptance. My teaching was also influenced by family therapy training and practice which emphasized the importance of connectedness and interrelatedness, an element missing in the individualism of humanism. One family work concept which was to have particular relevance for my teaching was Minuchin's (1974) concept of the therapist 'joining' the family, reducing the traditional distance between expert and client. Practice in a psychodynamically orientated psychiatric setting had helped me learn the skill of 'containment' (Bion 1970). The ability to be calmly receptive when difficult material is expressed is an essential skill for facilitating reflective learning (Pietroni 1994).

Then, crucially for me, came feminist pedagogy which provided a philosophical framework for bringing these elements together. Feminist principles in social work have been identified as having three core elements (Wetzel 1986). The first is the centrality of interpersonal relationships which emphasize a non-hierarchical, collaborative relationship. The second values the uniqueness of the individual and his/her subjective experience. The third principle is that of personal power and responsibility with a demystifying of the expert and a valuing of the contribution of all participants. No longer were students supposed to be blank slates for me to write on, they were to bring their experience into the classroom for them to build on.

When I returned to England in 1990, I was given the opportunity to step outside the practice of teaching and learning but to continue to consider it by evaluating Enquiry and Action Learning (EAL), an approach to social work education implemented in the Diploma in Social Work course at Bristol University. It is my research into EAL and my consequent thinking about facilitating learning which informs the balance of this chapter.

Enquiry and Action Learning

The name 'Enquiry and Action Learning' (EAL) was chosen to emphasize the process of learning through enquiry (seeking information through discovery) and action. The use of the term 'action learning' has been used somewhat differently elsewhere (Revans 1983; McGill and Beaty 1993) but there is a common theme of action as a continuous process of learning and reflection, where students learn with and from each other by working on real problems and reflecting on their experiences (McGill and Beaty 1993, p. 17). Within a framework of university and professional requirements the structure of the course is designed where possible to integrate principles of self-directedness (Burgess 1992). Educational theory suggests that knowledge has more significance when learnt through our own initiative and we learn best when we have been involved in setting the aims and objectives of learning (Knowles 1980; Kolb 1984).

To enable the reader to follow the discussion in this chapter, brief details about the course are included here. For more extensive detail see the book by

Hilary Burgess (1992), one of the course planners. EAL is a two-year full-time course leading to the professional qualification of the Diploma in Social Work awarded by the validating body, the Central Council for Education and Training in Social Work (CCETSW 1989). A combined total of eighty students, including graduates and non-graduates, are admitted per annum.

Lectures and seminars on discrete disciplines have been replaced by a problem-based learning approach where the 'study unit' is the focal point for learning. A study unit lasts on average for two weeks and is built around a case scenario drawn from practice. Topics for the study units are determined by course planners with input from students about their learning needs. Students decide which aspect of the scenario to work on according to individual and group learning needs. Study unit work is the core of the course. It is supplemented by about two lectures a week on theoretical frameworks, two workshops a term on aspects of anti-discriminatory practice, and a skills development programme. Students also undertake a supervised block placement in a social work agency in each of the two years.

Students work in 'study groups' of about ten students and group membership remains constant for approximately one term and always includes a mix of graduates and non-graduates. Membership in the first term is determined by course planners to ensure a balance of race and gender, and to ensure that where possible students who come from oppressed groups in society are not isolated in a study group. Membership of groups in subsequent terms introduces an element of choice reflecting students' learning preferences and choice of specialism.

Where possible students assume responsibility both individually and in groups for what they learn and how they learn. Each student group decides on and prioritizes the issues presented by the scenario and the knowledge and skill required to work on it. The group then decide how to tackle the work in the time available. Students may select learning activities from suggestions provided or design their own. In addition to dealing with learning tasks in relation to the problem at hand, groups reflect together on the process of learning and evaluate whether they have achieved their objectives. Group meetings are chaired by students themselves with help and guidance from a facilitator. In the interests of encouraging student self-directedness, as well as economy of resources, the facilitator attends approximately half the study unit meetings. The facilitator role is central at the beginning of the course and becomes increasingly peripheral as the course progresses. Facilitators are advised to be 'active but not directive. The essential tasks are enabling, listening, clarifying and guiding' (Course Handbook 1992).

Resources are provided to support self-directed learning. Students are given information about written, video and computer resources to which they have access, although these are inevitably limited by resource restrictions. Students may choose to consult named consultants drawn from both the university and practice. The timetable is planned to allow time for self-directed learning, with students having blocks of time when they can choose to work individually or collaboratively.

Within a framework of requirements, students have a wide range of choice about the content of their assessed work. The emphasis is on work which has a potential purpose beyond producing evidence for assessment. Students may therefore choose to submit briefing papers or presentations rather than conventional academic papers. Control of formal assessment has remained with staff, but it is planned to introduce elements of self and peer assessment as a central feature of assessed work.

Research into EAL

The approach taken to the evaluation is fully described elsewhere (Taylor 1993). For purposes of this discussion it may be useful for the reader to know that the research model was 'illuminative', a model developed to evaluate innovative educational programmes (Parlett and Hamilton 1972). The research objective was to describe and interpret the process of programme implementation and its implications for students and staff.

The methodology was primarily qualitative and ethnomedological as I immersed myself in the life of the course. The research subjects were the 14 staff (combined part-time and full-time) and the first cohort of 40 students who entered the course in 1990. The students were predominantly non-graduates, three-quarters of whom were women, with an average age of 35 and an age range of 23 to 53. Five students were black, the rest were white. The small cohort and high proportion of non-graduates was an outcome of the transition from an old to a new course. The experiences of the 1991 entry of 80 students were also evaluated to redress an imbalance in the first year towards non-graduates, and to understand how EAL was developing after the first year of implementation. The staff included four men and ten women, and with the exception of one black member, all staff were white.

A sample of nine students participated in audio-taped interviews throughout the course and in addition focus group interviews were held, open for all students to attend. All staff were interviewed individually prior to implementation and again on at least two consecutive occasions. There were also many opportunities to observe staff and students in formal and informal interactions. Practice Teachers of students in the sample were also interviewed. Some quantitative measures were used for triangulation purposes.

My objective was to research in 'partnership' with the staff (Whitaker and Archer 1994) and staff were actively involved in decisions about the research to ensure that the evaluation was utilization focused (Patton 1986). We collaborated on working out a research plan and I regularly discussed findings with staff for use in EAL development, as well as a means of checking findings and refocusing the research efforts. Early on, it was agreed with the staff that the facilitator role would be one focus of the research.

Theory of facilitating learning

In depth analysis of the facilitator role in self-directed learning is surprisingly sparse, perhaps proving Brookfield's point that in the adult learning literature we are in danger of ignoring the educator's role (Brookfield 1993). Boud (1987) conceptualizes the role of facilitator as planner and evaluator; as resource person; as learner centred; and as an instrument of social action and change. Jaques conceptualizes the style of the facilitator as responsive and reactive:

> It should not be supposed that the facilitator role represents a laissez-faire style of leadership; rather is there a sense of shared or developed responsibility for learning. It usually requires that the tutor be student centred, helping students express what they understand by respecting them for what they are rather than what they should be. (Jaques 1984, p. 147)

However, the challenge for the facilitator in social work education is that it is necessary but not sufficient to respect students for who they are and what they bring; there are also clear expectations that they assume the ideology of the profession and they develop specified knowledge, skills and values.

Brookfield discusses facilitation as a transactional dialogue between participants who each bring 'experiences, attitudinal sets, and alternative ways of looking at their personal, professional, political and recreational worlds' (Brookfield 1986, p. 23). This is an appealing way of viewing facilitation because if the educator has primary responsibility for student learning, this banking system of education (Freire 1981) disempowers the student. If, on the other hand, the student solely determines what is to be learnt and the educator simply responds, although this sounds admirably democratic it makes the facilitator into little more than a 'service manager' (Brookfield 1986, p. 21). Brookfield proposes that the role of facilitator is to participate fully and to 'challenge learners with alternative ways of interpreting their experiences and to present them with ideas and behaviours that cause them to examine critically their values, ways of acting and assumptions' (p. 23). In the research I was interested in examining the process and outcome of facilitating in this way.

Structuring and facilitating critical reflection

Boud and Knights (Chapter 2) propose that reflection must be grounded in the structure of the learning milieu. Before focusing on a discussion of transactional factors I will briefly review the structures designed to support reflection in EAL. These include: timetabled time, learning groups, problem-based learning, learning activities and reflective tools.

I Structuring reflective learning

The carefully planned structures outlined below are designed both to encourage reflection as well as self-directed learning. Many students become adept at using these structures to manage their own learning, and particularly towards the end of the course a facilitator may begin to feel like a service manager (Brookfield 1986).

Timetabled time Time for reflection is essential and must be included in the timetable. Time allocated for group meetings is designed to allow for learning activities which generate reflection. Time is also built into the timetable for individuals or sub-groups to use as they choose for their learning. This unstructured time presents students with a challenge to discipline themselves, particularly those students with caring responsibilities where for example it may be tempting to attend to personal matters rather than work with colleagues. Another risk, particularly for students today who face severe financial pressures, is that they use the time for part-time employment, in spite of course rules restricting this.

The study group Students remain in study groups for a term and a level of trust and connectedness develops which typically provides a relatively safe context in which the exploration essential to reflection can occur. Study groups do not always provide a safe environment; at worst they replicate the patterns of power and oppression in society at large and inhibit members from freely participating.

Problem-based learning As a structure problem-based learning provides opportunities for reflection of the kind which occur in practice, encouraging students to reflect on the knowledge, skills and values relevant to the 'problem' and on the relevance of their own experience. Students experience problem-based learning as highly relevant to practice and it engages their motivation to learn.

Learning activities Each study unit includes suggested learning activities and once students understand their value, they frequently design their own.

Learning activities typically combine the intellectual and affective, using techniques such as role plays, debates and panels to generate group reflection.

Reflective tools Related to learning activities are reflective tools which provide students with a means of structuring reflection. For example, early in the course the Personal Learning Profile provides a structure for students to record their relevant personal and professional pre-course experiences, and begin to determine their objectives for the course. Aspects of the profile may be shared by students with their study groups.

II Facilitating reflective learning

If the task of facilitator is simply to put structures to enable learning into place, then the role of facilitator would be little more than service manager. However, as Sophie Freud (1988) suggests at the beginning of this chapter, the facilitator must enter into a relationship with students and use interactional skills to facilitate reflective learning. Research into EAL indicates that there are different requirements for facilitating reflective learning at different stages of the course, there are also some specific areas for the facilitator to address in facilitating critical reflexivity, facilitating public/private reflection, and facilitation and power. Finally, there are some issues specific to facilitating the learning of 'non-traditional' students.

Facilitating reflection at different stages of the course The role of the facilitator changes over the life of the course. At the beginning of the course, with few exceptions, students seek direction, feeling lost and looking for someone to modulate their environment (Taylor 1993). Even for mature students who may have been used to functioning in a self-directed way in their pre-course lives, this does not necessarily transfer into the capacity for self-directed learning in education (Brookfield 1986).

Perry (1970) constructed a model of intellectual development describing how students' concepts of knowledge and of themselves as learners changes over time. In the early stages students view the world from a position of basic duality where understanding is seen as right or wrong and the teacher is expected to provide answers. The role of the facilitator is to begin to help students become aware of the absence of such truths and to appreciate the diversity of opinion and perspectives. This can be a disorientating process which may cause confusion, anxiety and anger (Salzberger-Wittenberg et al 1983; Brundage and Mackeracher 1980). Students may handle these feelings by appearing dependent or counter-dependent (Brundage and Mackeracher 1980). The challenge for the facilitator is to help the students contain these feelings so they do not become overwhelming and inhibit learning. It is not easy to contain difficult feelings which can gather momentum in a group, and when confronted with student anxiety and frustration it can be tempting to move towards more structure and certainty, although facilitators with group work experience may find it easier to manage than those without.

The theme of stages of development is also central to the literature on learning in groups (Abercrombie 1983; Jaques 1984). Initially the role of the facilitator is central and as the group develops, it shifts towards being more peripheral. As groups change membership each term there is an initial period of disorientation as students respond to being in a new group, but over the two years of the course this disorientation diminishes and they are increasingly able to manage the group themselves. Facilitators become less central and facilitating a first term group is very different from a final term group.

It is common for students entering social work education to feel pressured and in addition initial experience with self-directed learning can be alarming. As this student reflected on her experience at the beginning of the course,

> I actually wanted someone to point me in the right direction rather than say go out and find out for yourself . . . I felt as if I was in the sea really and the people around me were also floating in the sea and no-one really knew what we were doing.

An early research finding was that students felt that an orientation to EAL would be useful (Taylor and Burgess 1995). In part this could be provided to the total student group for example by giving a lecture about the philosophy and structure of EAL, in an attempt to increase students' conceptual understanding of EAL. Students' 'willingness to accept increased (learner) control will depend on whether or not, in any particular case, they judge it to be a valid strategy and a situation from which they can learn' (Candy 1987, p. 174). However, the predominant work of understanding how to learn and reflect is done 'on the job' in study group work with facilitators guiding the process.

Facilitating critical reflexivity   Facilitators were advised to be 'active but not directive' (Course Handbook 1992–1994) but the boundary between activity and directiveness is difficult to determine. Initially some facilitators were concerned about the risk of being directive and disempowering students. As one facilitator said, 'My practice was to be so concerned about accepting student power and responsibility . . . that I underestimated what I had to offer them'. Students hesitate to offer each other critical feedback and the risk develops of students and the facilitator colluding to avoid expression of difference. Yet, the facilitator must actively grapple with pressures towards group conformity (Pietroni 1994) and the process of exploring and reflecting on experiences must include a level of critical analysis or it will be little more than anecdotal reminiscences (Usher and Bryant 1989).

Experiences must be submitted to two forms of critical review. First, formal theory is a resource, a way of bringing critical analysis to bear on inductively derived situational insights; secondly, assumptions which are derived from experience can be subjected to collaborative scrutiny (Brookfield 1993, p. 31). One technique to stimulate critical reflection and challenge taken for granted assumptions is to ask questions (Jaques 1984; Brookfield 1986). These may be questions which require learners to link their explorations to existing research or frameworks of knowledge. Good questions may be regarded 'as gifts rather than intrusive assault' (Sophie Freud 1988, p. 110) and the facilitator has the opportunity to model this skill.

One effective strategy for determining an appropriate level of activity is for facilitators to negotiate their role with the group and check out what is helpful. There was some agreement among students that a successful facilitator contributed from the back seat (Taylor 1994):

> She took a back seat and we had to work it out amongst ourselves but we did pick her brains when we needed it, her particular expertise. She was really coming in when we asked her and occasionally she might contribute subtly . . . from the back seat.

Facilitating public/private reflection   Reflecting on experience often generates difficult feelings. Painful personal experiences may become reactivated and there is some evidence from recent American research that the incidence of dysfunction in the family of origin of social work students is higher than on some other professional education courses such as business (Black, Jefferys and Hartley 1993; Russel et al 1993). Students are often working in placements with situations which involve pain and the facilitator may need to help the student and the group contain their difficult feelings. Pietroni (1994) in her discussion of reflective learning in social work education emphasizes the importance of Bion's work (1970) and the value of allowing 'painful truths' to emerge.

One vivid example of learning from personal experience occurred in a study group session focusing on mental health. A black student poignantly described her experience of a family member diagnosed as paranoid schizophrenic who had become a victim of the criminal justice system, as well as caused turmoil for his family. The story had significant impact on the group, creating opportunities for learning which rarely arise from pursuing such material simply on a cognitive level. Telling the story also had an impact on the individual student who became overwhelmed with her feelings. The facilitator was able to make connections between the experience of the individual student and research about the discriminatory response of the mental health and criminal justice systems to black men with mental health problems, thus underlining the structural issues involved and contributing to group learning but at the same time depathologizing the issue for the individual student.

This particular facilitator was comfortable with the expression of strong feelings. It can be tempting for facilitators to intervene early on in such a disclosure and curtail the telling of the story, denying the value of feelings as a legitimate source of knowledge. It is also tempting to succumb to the pressures of a timetable and move on. This kind of scenario is frequently encountered in practice in situations which are far more unpredictable; in the classroom they offer a valuable opportunity for the facilitator to model a response.

The other learning opportunity embedded in this kind of experience is the negotiation which must take place with the learning group about the complexities of confidentiality. Early in the course the facilitator takes a central role in negotiating rules of confidentiality and, as the course progresses, students take the lead on this issue themselves. As with containing feelings, this is also an important opportunity for the facilitator to model practice.

Reflection and power   In education, the teacher traditionally holds power as an expert, in addition to holding assessment power. EAL facilitators do not necessarily have subject expertise in the topics of the study units, and they are not in a position of formally assessing (grading) members of their study groups. Nevertheless, they are in positions of power which in turn has implications for reflective learning.

How should facilitators manage their subject expertise? When EAL was first implemented, facilitators were concerned about being generalists in relation to study unit themes, in particular about their capacity to respond if there were gaps in students' work, or if students appeared to be taking the 'wrong' approach. Such concern has lessened as facilitators realized they could reflect with students, and this provides an important means for joining with them. The opportunity to be the learner with students as well as the facilitator is a powerful joining device at the same time as being satisfying for a facilitator who is learning about areas new to him/her.

As an expert on the topic of the study unit, facilitators face the temptation of presenting a seminar and short circuiting the process of student reflection. The prospect of the facilitator as a blank slate is unappealing to facilitators and students, and for authentic dialogue and discourse to take place students must get to know the facilitator (Freire 1981; Mezirow 1983). This includes knowing the work facilitators have done and the fields they have worked in. Brookfield (1993) suggests that facilitators must earn the right to ask others to share their experiences by being ready to share their own. As

EAL facilitators become more confident in their role they also develop confidence in contributing their subject expertise.

In addition to expert power, facilitators hold assessment power. Although facilitators are not in the position of formally grading students in the group, students are aware facilitators carry other staff roles, including an assessment role, and consequently monitor their behaviour accordingly. The facilitator also represents the profession in that the course is accredited by a validating body and some behaviours which are not congruent with course requirements are not acceptable. For example, student attendance at study groups is a requirement for which students are expected to be accountable.

Effective facilitating includes clarifying power issues and making them explicit in the group so that they operate at the least restrictive level in relation to learning. By explicitly addressing issues of power, facilitators are modelling how power issues may be handled in practice. So far the discussion has been about formal power but equally, if not more significant, is the informal power held by majority groups. In the next section of this chapter I discuss the 'non-traditional' students, often from a disadvantaged minority, who have left school with minimum qualifications and entered university via routes such as Access.

Facilitating reflective learning for 'non-traditional' students In addition to being responsive to the different stages of readiness of students for self-directedness, facilitators need to be aware of the influence of differences in gender, race and class in student readiness to reflect. Based on research into the ways white and black women learn, Belenky et al (1986) proposed five stages of epistemological development for women. The first two stages appear to exclude possibilities for reflection. The first stage is 'silence, a position in which women experience themselves as mindless and voiceless and subject to the whims of external authority'. The second is 'received knowledge, a perspective from which women conceive of themselves as capable of receiving, even reproducing, knowledge from the all-knowing external authorities but not capable of creating knowledge on their own' (Belenky et al 1986, p. 15). Women become progressively more aware and accepting of their own voices in the three subsequent stages: the stage of subjective knowledge where students realize there are many interpretations of ideas and events; the stage of procedural knowledge where students begin to formulate a structure which will allow them to convey ideas; and the final stage where students create new knowledge.

The implications for the facilitator are that in the early stages of the course a crucial task is specifically working with women to help them recognize their contributions and abilities (Taylor and Burgess 1995). A reward for the facilitator is being part of a process where women students increasingly gain confidence in their capacities, 'building a sense of personal empowerment which results in a new perception of self as leader' (Dore 1994, p. 101).

There is less research into the impact of cultural differences on adult learning. In her study of black social work students Rosen found evidence that they began the course as if they 'were entering unknown territory and feeling their way blindfolded through what they understood to be a minefield, intended to explode their aspirations at the first chance' (Rosen 1993, p. 182). This pattern was also found in a small exploratory study of Bristol students who fell into a non-traditional category, having left school with four GSCEs or less and made their way into higher education through non-traditional routes, including Access courses. The black students, in common with working-class students, shared the experience of feeling they were in the wrong place and did not belong. The disjuncture experienced by these students can be significant (Weil 1988) which requires facilitators to be particularly active in managing this:

> Enabling teachers and groups can go a long way to counteract the impact of disjunction arising from forces that seem outside the bounds of one person's agency, and to create an oasis of integration in which the experience of other kinds of disjunction can be made sense of and effectively managed. (Weil 1989, p. 143)

Studies of non-traditional learners suggest that the facilitator's relationship with the learner is central in the creation of the 'oasis' referred to by Weil. Pye (1991) suggests returners begin to succeed when they experience optimism and interest from their teachers, in contrast to the students' previous experience of teachers who were impatient, bored and sarcastic. Mills and Molloy (1989) found that staff readiness to welcome non-standard entrants and a willingness and competence to respond to their needs was crucial. Rosen (1993) found that personal contact between students and staff was important.

Facilitators are not presented with clear-cut requests for contact. Non-traditional students who are likely to have had negative experiences in the past with teachers, or with people in a position of power and authority, face a significant dilemma in seeking help: 'Who could they trust with their uncertainties without being labelled as failing?' (Rosen 1993, p. 179). This anxiety was also expressed by the non-traditional EAL students who were afraid of appearing stupid or of being rebuffed if they sought help. In these circumstances it is tempting for the facilitator who is dealing with many academic demands on his/her time to be available if help is sought, but to ignore indirect signs that help is needed.

Facilitating learning and modelling practice

Early in this chapter I described my attempts to integrate practice skills into teaching and facilitating. Throughout the chapter I have referred to parallels between facilitating learning and practice, both areas where we use our skills in order to try and make a difference (Freud 1988). There are obvious limits to this comparison which must not be overdrawn. For example, many service users are not voluntary, whereas students generally are. However, a central similarity is that in both facilitating learning and practice, I learn from and with the student/service user, as well as clearly having a role and responsibility as facilitator. An ultimate objective of the process for both students and service users is for them to become independent. As a student completing the course commented on looking back:

> I feel that staff have actually played a very small part in my course but then perhaps that's how it should be in an EAL course.

We cannot predict with certainty but we can safely speculate that students prepared for self-directed reflective learning are prepared for the rapid changes they will encounter in practice today and the requirements for life-long learning.

Note

The author would like to thank the Halley Stewart Trust for funding the research which enabled this chapter to be written.

References

Bion, W. (1970), *Attention and Interpretation*. London: Tavistock Publications.

Black, P.N., Jefferys, D. and Hartley, E.K. (1993), 'Personal History of Psychosocial Trauma in the Early Life of Social Work and Business Students', *Journal of Social Work Education*, **29** (2), 171–80.

Boud, D. (1987), 'A facilitator's view of adult learning', in D. Boud and V. Griffin (eds), *Appreciating Adults Learning from the Adult Perspective*. London: Kogan Page.

Boud, D. (1988), 'Moving towards autonomy', in D. Boud (ed.), *Developing Student Autonomy in Learning*. London: Routledge, Kegan Paul.

Boud, D., Keogh, R. and Walker, D. (eds) (1985), *Reflection: Turning Experience into Learning*. London: Kogan Page.

Brookfield, S. (1986), *Understanding and Facilitating Adult Learning*. Milton Keynes: Open University Press.

Brookfield, S. (1993), 'Through the lens of learning: how the visceral experience of learning reframes teaching', in D. Boud, R. Cohen and D. Walker (eds), *Using Experience for Learning*. Buckingham: SRHE and Open University Press.

Burgess, H. (1992), *Problem-Led Learning for Social Work: The Enquiry and Action Approach*. London: Whiting and Birch.

Candy, P. (1987), 'Evolution, revolution or devolution: increasing learner control in the instructional setting', in D. Boud and V. Griffin (eds), *Appreciating Adults Learning from the Adult Perspective*. London: Kogan Page.

Candy, P. (1991), *Self-Direction for Lifelong Learning*. San Francisco: Jossey Bass.

Central Council for Education and Training in Social Work (1989), *Requirements and Regulations for the Diploma in Social Work*, Paper 30. London: CCETSW.

Course Handbook (1992–1994), Bristol: University of Bristol, Department of Social Work.

Cowan, J. (1993), Paper presented at 'Professionals for the 21st Century: Active Learning for Professional Education' Conference, Bristol University.

Dore, M. (1994), 'Feminist Pedagogy and the Teaching of Social Work Practice', *Journal of Social Work Education*, **30** (1), 97–106.

Freire, P. (1981), *Pedagogy of the Oppressed*. New York: Herder and Herder.

Freud, S. (1988), *My Three Mothers and Other Passions*. New York: New York University Press.

Jaques, D. (1984), *Learning in Groups*. London: Croom Helm.

Knowles, M. (1980), *The Modern Practice of Adult Education: From Andragogy to Pedagogy*. Chicago: Follett.

Kolb, D. (1984), *Experiential Learning: Experience as a Source of Learning and Development*. New Jersey: Prentice Hall.

McGill, I. and Beaty, L. (1993), *Action Learning: A Practitioner's Guide*. London: Kogan Page.

Mezirow, J. (1983), 'A critical theory of adult learning and education', in M. Tight, (ed.), *Adult Learning and Education: A Reader*. London: Croom Helm.

Mills, A. and Molloy, S. (1989), 'Experiencing the Experienced: the Impact of Non-Standard Entrants upon a Programme of Higher Education', *Studies in Higher Education*, **14** (1), 41–54.

Minuchin, S. (1974), *Families and Family Therapy*. Cambridge, Mass: Harvard University Press.

Parlett, M. and Hamilton, D. (1972), *Evaluation as Illumination: A New Approach to the Study of Innovatory Programmes*. Edinburgh: University of Edinburgh.

Patton, M. (1986), *Utilisation-Focused Evaluation*. London: Sage.

Perry, W. (1970), *Forms of Intellectual and Ethical Development in College Years*. New York: Holt, Rinehart and Winston.

Pietroni, M. (1994), 'The nature and aims of professional education for social workers: a postmodern perspective', in M. Yelloly and M. Henkel (eds), *Learning and Teaching in Social Work: Towards Reflective Practice*. London: Kingsley.

Pye J. (1991), *Second Chances*. Oxford: Oxford University Press.

Revans, R. (1983), *Action Learning: New Techniques for Action Learning*. London: Blond and Briggs.

Rogers, C. (1982), *On Becoming a Person*. London: Constable.

Rosen, V. (1993), 'Black students in higher education', in M. Thorpe, R. Edwards and A. Hanson (eds), *Culture and Processes of Adult Learning: A Reader*. London: Routledge and the Open University.

Russel, R., Gill, P., Coyne, A. and Woody, J. (1993), 'Dysfunction in the Family of Origin of MSW and Other Graduate Students', *Journal of Social Work Education*, **29** (1), 121–9.

Salzberger-Wittenberg I., Henry, G. and Osborne, E. (1983), *The Emotional Experience of Teaching and Learning*. London: Routledge and Kegan Paul.

Schön, D. (1983), *The Reflective Practitioner*. New York: Basic Books.

Schön D. (1987), *Educating the Reflective Practitioner*. San Francisco: Jossey Bass.

Taylor, I. (1993), 'A Case for Social Work Evaluation of Social Work Education', *British Journal of Social Work*, **23** (2),123–38.

Taylor, I. (1994) 'From the Back Seat: Facilitating Self-directed Learning in a Social Work Course', *Issues in Social Work Education*, **14** (1), 18–38.

Taylor, I. and Burgess, H. (1995), 'Orientation to Self-directed Learning: Paradox or Paradigm?', *Studies in Higher Education*, **20** (1), 87–98.

Usher, R. and Bryant, I. (1989), *Adult Education in Theory, Practice and Research: The Captive Triangle*. London: Routledge.

Weil, S. (1988), 'From a Language of Observation to a Language of Experience: Studying the Perspectives of Diverse Adults in Higher Education', *Journal of Access Studies*, **3** (1), 17–43.

Weil, S. (1989), 'Access: towards education or miseducation? Adults imagine the future', in O. Fulton (ed.), *Access and Institutional Change*. Milton Keynes: SRHE and Open University Press.

Wetzel, J. (1986), 'A Feminist World View Conceptual Framework', *Social Casework*, 1986, March, 166–73.

Whitaker, D.S. and Archer, L. (1994), 'Partnership Research and its Contribution to Team Building', *Social Work Education*, **13** (3), 39–60.

8 'Patterns that connect': opportunities for reflective practice in network placements

Jane Batchelor and Karen Boutland

A central required component of all professional social work training courses in the UK is the placement. It provides the setting in which students both learn about and demonstrate their competence to practise. Comparing the potential of different types of placements and different supervision arrangements, for enhancing transfer of learning, has particular relevance to a discussion of reflective practice. There are influential variables operating in placements that are likely to enhance or diminish their potential to provide a context conducive to developing as a reflective practitioner, yet little has been written about the organizational context within which such learning takes place. Our research on a particular placement model (Boutland and Batchelor 1993) has provided us with detailed material on the experiences of students and practice teachers, some of which sheds light on these contextual variables and their influence on students' development as reflective practitioners.

Most social work students still undertake each placement within one team or work group of a single agency or organization. Although the private social work sector, which mainly provides residential and day care services for adults, has grown rapidly in recent years, at present limited use is made of it for student placements. Placements are usually located solely in either the statutory or voluntary (not for profit) sector. Within statutory agencies such as Social Services Departments and the Probation Service, employees' and students' roles and responsibilities are largely determined by the legislation which they are employed to implement and by the policies and procedures of the bureaucracies within which they are employed. By contrast voluntary organizations are free from statutory responsibilities and so can determine their own terms of reference. There is the potential for workers to participate actively in the process of developing, managing and implementing policy and practice in their organization, often working in close collaboration with service users.

Whether placed in the statutory or voluntary sector, students will usually have a practice teacher who is a member of the team or work group in which they are placed. However if no worker with appropriate social work and practice teaching qualifications is available, a 'long-arm' practice teacher from another setting or agency may be appointed. In such cases the student will still have an identified supervisor in their placement setting, responsible for their day-to-day practice. The role of the long-arm practice teacher is to coordinate the student's learning experience in the placement, assess their competence and compile the placement report, with the day-to-day supervisor contributing to all of these. Whatever the practice teaching arrangements, students are placed within a single agency context or setting for the duration of each placement.

The nature of network placements

In contrast to the traditional single location arrangement, network placements are becoming more common. We are using the term 'network' here to indicate an organizational or contextual network. A network placement is a flexible type of practice placement that reaches across professional boundaries and agency settings. A single network placement will have various component parts which are connected, whether by user group, by method or by context of the work. For example, a placement might span the voluntary and statutory sectors, with a student working part of each week in a family centre run by a national children's charity, and the remainder of the week in the local Social Services child care team from which some of the referrals to the family centre originate. One feature of such placements is their flexibility; they have the potential to offer a variety of experiences according to the student's individual learning needs. Although network placements may have been created initially in response to a shortage of suitable single-location placements, they have gradually been identified as offering distinct advantages to students, practice teachers and organizations.

Early in the 1990s we undertook a piece of research to evaluate network placements (Boutland and Batchelor 1993). We built directly upon earlier work by Boutland and Baldwin (1991) on placement development, in which they had proposed a model of network placements and postulated the advantages and disadvantages of the model from the position of students, tutors and practice teachers. In our work we set out to test their hypotheses by asking those who had been party to such placements for their views based on their experiences to date.

Researching advantages and drawbacks to network placements

Our study focused on placements used by three local, full-time, college-based professional social work courses in the south west of England. The three courses had a total intake of approximately 165 students per year, with each student undertaking two placements over two years. From contact with social work tutors on the three courses, we identified that thirty-six network placements had recently been undertaken by local social work students. For our research, we set out to gather information on the process of these placements. In addition we sought the general views of the students, their practice teachers and their tutors on the overall potential of the network model. Did they think that more such placements should be developed in the future?

Of the fifty-eight practice teachers and placement supervisors involved in the network placements in our study, forty-eight were traced, interviewed and completed questionnaires (as detailed in Boutland and Batchelor 1993). Twenty-eight of the students who had undertaken these placements were traced, of whom seventeen returned completed questionnaires. There did not appear to be any bias in the sample of students who responded, in terms of the proportion of male and female students, and of black and white students. In addition, questionnaires were sent out to the social work tutors currently working on the three college courses. Of those who responded, ten had recently tutored students on network placements.

The overlap of network placements experienced by the tutors, students and practice teachers who participated in our research yielded complete data on twenty-eight placements in all. Over half of these placements were totally in the statutory sector, often linking field work with a group care setting. Eight spanned the statutory and voluntary sector, and just three were solely in voluntary organizations. The majority comprised two component parts, with most students splitting their time equally between the two locations each week. However over half of the students had a 'long-arm' practice teacher who was located in a third setting; that is, in one of the three Practice Learning Centres in the region. On the basis of responses from practice teachers and students, it was possible to determine the main focus of the work undertaken in the network placements. For the majority, the 'pattern' that connected the components of the network was the user group with which students were working. Twelve of the placements were in child care, four in mental health, four in adult care; and eight were described as 'generic'. For some of these eight, connections between the elements of the network were not apparent, suggesting they may have been created from a 'rag bag' of settings, possibly in the face of a shortage of singleton placements.

Whilst our research (Boutland and Batchelor 1993) tested the full range of advantages and drawbacks of network placements hypothesized by Boutland and Baldwin (1991), for the purposes of this discussion of reflective practice we are focusing on some of those relating to students. Boutland and Baldwin anticipated network placements would open up a wide variety of learning opportunities for students, enhancing the potential for transfer of learning. Components of the network could be contracted or expanded according to individual students' needs. This suggested two questions for us to address, in our evaluation of network placements from the point of view of students. How did the range of learning opportunities available in the network placements, including opportunities for students to demonstrate anti-discriminatory and anti-racist practice, compare with the range available in singleton placements? Was transfer of learning facilitated for those students?

Another of Boutland and Baldwin's hypotheses was that evidence of a student's practice competence from a network would provide a more complete picture of the student. They anticipated there would be more opportunities for students to demonstrate, and practice teachers to gather, evidence of competence in networks than in singleton placements, resulting in a more holistic assessment. We also wanted to find out whether there was any support for Boutland and Baldwin's hypotheses (1991) that drawbacks to network placements might include a risk that students could experience incongruent styles of working across the network placements, that lines of accountability in network placements could be unclear, and that students could feel either unsupported or, at the other extreme, oversupervised.

In responding to our questions we asked those students, tutors and practice teachers who had experience of both network and singleton placements to comment on the former in the light of their knowledge and experience of the latter. In addition we asked their general views on the potential and the drawbacks of the network model. Responses to some of these questions (such as those about transfer of learning) have direct relevance to the development of the student as a reflective practitioner. Responses to other questions help our understanding of the positives and negatives of network placements, thus putting us in a better position to evaluate the broad potential of the model for enhancing all social work students' development as reflective practitioners. Thus this material is incorporated in the following discussion.

The value of network placements

The unanimous response from practice teachers and supervisors was that the network placements in which they had been directly involved offered increased learning opportunities for students, including greater opportunities for students to develop skills in and demonstrate anti-discriminatory practice. The majority of students who were in a position to compare single-ton and network placements concurred with these views. However it was recognized by students and practice teachers alike that these advantages could be at the cost of depth of placement experience, unless placements are carefully planned and students' learning monitored throughout. As one student commented, 'If closely linked settings or closely related agencies are involved, the potential [of a network placement] is massive. If not, the result can be negative, in that the student gets a sample of each but not a great deal of experience in either'.

The Central Council for Education and Training in Social Work, which validates professional social work programmes in the UK, has specified that qualifying social workers must be able to transfer knowledge and skills to new situations (CCETSW 1991). Thus social work students are expected to develop and demonstrate in the course of their training their ability to transfer learning from one setting or area of work to another. Of the practice teachers interviewed for the research, four out of every five considered their network placements had facilitated the students' transfer of learning. The remaining practice teachers did not suggest that the network placements had hindered transfer of learning by students, but rather that facilitation or hindrance had depended on factors other than the type of placement. One tutor observed that network placements '. . . potentially facilitate [transfer of learning], but it is easy to assume transfer is taking place just by virtue of the experience, which it may not be'. A variable identified by some of the practice teachers as influential was the student's ability to transfer, suggesting they saw such an ability as fixed and not open to improvement. However, others noted the important role of the practice teacher in helping students develop their ability to transfer learning. As one tutor commented, 'It needs a skilful practice teacher to help students make the connections'.

From the students' comments it was clear that they could identify skills they had learned and transferred across the networks. Some gave examples such as transferring interviewing, counselling and family therapy skills. One cited drawing on learning from participation at case conferences in a field work setting to multidisciplinary meetings in a group care setting in the other part of the network. Finally, one student whose placement encompassed work in a voluntary organization and in a statutory agency described transferring learning about principles of social work practice. This student wrote, 'Working in statutory and voluntary agencies at the same time meant the values of one . . . could be transferred to my working with Social Services clients, working in partnership with rather than for the client'.

To summarize, the experience of those who had participated in network placements was that they had provided enhanced opportunities for transfer of learning compared with singleton placements. However, it cannot be assumed that this transfer will happen of its own accord. Although a student who has already developed abilities in this area may make good use, unaided, of the enhanced opportunities available in network placements, all students will benefit from the skills of a practice teacher in developing their ability to transfer learning.

Although practice teachers, tutors and students found that students were more likely to experience different styles of working across a network than a singleton placement, in general this was viewed positively. They considered these differences potentially helped rather than hindered students' learning, as students had opportunities to see different workers either approaching similar tasks in different ways, or having a different focus (e.g. that of a voluntary organization compared with that of a statutory agency), and transfer such learning from one element of the placement to another. One practice teacher, reflecting on the network placement model, commented: '. . . the student can achieve good work without dependency on "the right way". It is good to see different styles'. However it was also acknowledged that differences in working styles could be very demanding on students. Close collaboration between those supervising the various components of the network and the overall practice teacher was seen as necessary to ensure that the student had the opportunity to learn from rather than just be confused by such differences. As one tutor responded, 'On reflection I feel transfer of learning across styles could have been addressed explicitly'. Transfer of learning by students may be hindered if these differences are not acknowledged, reflected upon and understood. The role of the practice teacher is central to this process; clearly they must be cognisant with the styles of working across the component elements of the network to help the student in this process. When these conditions are fulfilled, network placements again provide rich opportunities for students to develop as reflective practitioners.

Views on the network model in general

The findings discussed so far are based in the main on the specific experiences of students, practice teachers and tutors. However we also wanted their reflections on the network placement model in general. On the theme of the potential of the network placement model for students' skill development, there were positive comments from practice teachers in a range of settings. One commented: 'Network placements are ideal training for workers in the field of child protection and ongoing (treatment) work, where interagency collaboration, and where understanding of attitudes in other agencies is essential, and where the focus of another part of the system is important. E.g. work with children compared to work with abusers/perpetrators'. Another practice teacher made an observation regarding their relevance to future practice, stating 'More network placements will be needed in the future as that is the type of work which social work in the adult care field will be moving towards'.

The potential of the network placement model was seen by students in terms of the learning opportunities available, and their own personal development. One commented: 'They give the opportunity to experience a variety of work settings and to compare and contrast the two. They cram a lot of opportunities into a fairly short time – this may be the only time the student has the luxury to "sample" an area of work which might hold an interest for the future'. Another student stated, 'With network placements the student is able to be more proactive and take responsibility for creating opportunities for learning. In area offices in a singleton placement – the work is just there'. However some students qualified their comments about such placements. For example, one stated that the potential was '. . . enormous, as long as they are managed well . . . and the placement supervisors are prepared to work together and not compete for the student's time/attention'. Another wrote, 'With careful planning and due recognition for the added complexity of network placements I think they should be offered to more students.'

In their comments, tutors also acknowledged the potential for broadening the student's awareness and skills in a network placement, through experience of different social work roles and the opportunities to experience interprofessional and inter-agency work. In particular the network placement model was identified as offering learning opportunities that reflect the changing reality of social work.

In summary, whatever the specific experiences of those involved in network placements, when reflecting on the overall potential of the network model, they considered such placements would provide a greater range or variety of learning opportunities for students. This was their view for all types of network placements, but particularly so for those that spanned a voluntary organization and statutory agency. The network placement model provides opportunities for students to learn more about multidisciplinary work and interagency cooperation, through work with different user groups, using different styles of work and learning how different parts of an agency work with (or against) each other. Students can gain confidence in their ability to liaise with a wide variety of people. For example, in one multidisciplinary setting the student saw different aspects of the care process, from the perspective of a psychologist, a district nurse and the home aides. Managing a network placement, a student can show a capability and flexibility that may not be possible to demonstrate in a single setting. At the same time it was recognized that network placements are a challenge for students. They have to learn to be excellent managers of time, having direct experience of prioritizing their work and learning to use decision making and assertiveness skills.

Returning to Boutland and Baldwin's (1991) hypotheses, they had antici-pated some drawbacks as well as benefits accruing from network place-ments. An anticipated drawback was the increased risk that accountability for students' work would be unclear, compared with the risk in singleton placements. It was felt this would diminish the value of network placements as students might experience either feeling unsupported or oversupervised. In practice this was not the experience of the majority of students and prac-tice teachers who comprised our sample. Most found lines of accountability clear in their network placements. Even if there was some confusion at the outset about who was accountable for what, this was soon resolved. However, when asked to reflect generally on the network placement model, the potential for problems to arise when the parties involved are unsure of their own and each other's roles and responsibilities were highlighted, even by those who had not had this negative experience themselves. As there are more 'actors' in a network than in a singleton placement, the potential for confusion is greater and thus every care must be taken at the outset to ensure that all are clear where the various placement responsibilities rest.

Regarding assessment of students and the evidencing of that assessment, our research supports Boutland and Baldwin's hypotheses that both are enhanced in network placements. The majority of practice teachers and tutors had found that so long as the placement was carefully set up, with assessment responsibilities clarified at the outset, the assessment process in a network placement was fairer than that in a singleton placement. In addition most found network placements offered more opportunities for them to col-lect evidence of the student's competence. This was particularly related to opportunities for direct observation of the student's practice. Often one part of the network would provide naturally occurring opportunities to observe the student (e.g. in a group care setting) that were less readily available in other parts of the network.

The experiences of the students of assessment and evidencing on their net-work placements were somewhat different from those of practice teachers and tutors. Although few students had cited problems regarding under-standing lines of accountability for their work, it appeared that lines of accountability for their assessment were less often clear to them. Most reported that their network placements had provided more opportunities for evidencing their competence than their singleton placements, but one student experienced difficulties. This student commented: 'I was spending less time with each placement supervisor and doing less than a full place-ment's work for each, yet had to prove my competence to both'.

When students, practice teachers and tutors were asked to reflect gener-ally on the potential drawbacks of the model, more potential areas of concern were identified than had actually been experienced by them in the network placements. The potential for problems to arise when the parties involved are unsure of their own and each other's roles and responsibilities were highlighted, even by those who had not had this negative experience themselves. Attention was also drawn to the relatively high workload likely to be faced by students, tutors and practice teachers in setting up and maintaining network placements. Despite these potential drawbacks, the overall view was that the network placement model has great potential, particularly because such placements provide students with enhanced learning opportunities.

Reflective practice in network placements

Our research and initial analysis of the network placement model (Boutland and Batchelor 1993) did not specifically examine the potential of the model in terms of students' opportunities for reflection, although such opportunities had been anticipated by Boutland and Baldwin. However, our findings suggest that network placements do provide excellent opportunities for reflection, due to the particular position and role of the practice teachers in such placements, combined with the enhanced learning opportunities available to students.

Beginning with the role of the practice teacher in developing reflective practice, some features of network placements may hinder whilst others may help them in this regard. As already noted, there may be risks that students in network placements will gain breadth at the expense of depth of experience, and get lost in the complexity of the placement. However, with sound practice teaching these factors can be turned to an advantage, as students are enabled to reflect on their own and others' practice. In the context of supervision, all students can be provided with a boundaried space in which to make sense of, and reflect on experiences. For those students in network placements, they have a practice teacher who inevitably works at one remove from at least some of the network, potentially enhancing the process of reflection in supervision. The focus is upon common learning across the components of the placement, including reflection on the ways in which learning from experiences in one part of the placement might here and now be transferred across to another part. Although all students are encouraged to transfer and apply learning from one experience to another, the opportunity for reflection on action followed by transfer of learning may be less readily available to students on singleton placements. For most they will have to wait until their next placement or employment to test out such learning from experience in new practice settings.

In discussing the ways in which social work education is relevant to Schön's (1983) work on the concept of the reflective practitioner, Papell and Skolnik (1992, p. 24) note that 'the ethical and value dilemmas confronted in social work practice require practitioners to reflect on their actions'. As discussed above, in network placements the practice teacher will inevitably be at 'arm's length' from at least part of the network in which the student is placed, so is well positioned to enable the student to talk about and reflect on such dilemmas, whilst being personally distanced. The day-to-day placement supervisors in the work setting (or on-site practice teachers in singleton placements) may be closely involved in the very issues which students raise, making it hard for them to be able to take a meta-position, and so limiting the extent to which they can facilitate their students' learning in this regard.

It is not only important that there are opportunities created by practice teachers for students to reflect on their practice. The content of that reflection should not be ignored. In her analysis of pre-service education programmes for teachers in training in the USA, Valli (1993) warns against trivialized, narrowly focused reflection. This warning applies equally to social workers in training. Practice teachers of social work students in network placements are well placed to help those students reflect on wider issues, such as those relating to social work ethics, that may be common to their practice across various elements of the network. In addition, students on network placements have at least two people involved in their supervision, potentially increasing the opportunities for reflection.

Turning to the relationship between the enhanced learning opportunities in network placements and developing as a reflective practitioner, it is important that social work students are prepared for the wide variety of contexts within which they might eventually be employed, and to the changing world in which they will practise (Webber 1992–1993). As Pietroni (1995, p. 49) has observed, 'The constant flux and reorganisation of social services require of professionals that they are able to reframe their knowledge, skills and practices into new combinations and categories to suit a world where skill-mixes of a radically new kind are required and ethical dilemmas are often profound'. Whilst no training programme can ever cover all possible contexts (nor would this necessarily be desirable even if it were feasible) students who undertake network placements have opportunities within those placements to experience and reflect upon a wider range of contexts than students undertaking singleton placements. This is particularly true for the students whose network placements incorporate work in the smaller voluntary organizations.

Small voluntary organizations may not be able to provide full-time singleton placements, as they often have very low staffing levels, with restricted opportunities for staff to undertake practice teacher training. Yet they offer a managerial climate which Day (1993, p. 88) has suggested is essential for successful professional development; namely a 'climate of collaboration and consultation in which staff [and students] are actively involved in decision-making and in which they feel valued'. In this way a student can experience an organizational culture very different from that of the bureaucratic setting of a Social Services Department or the Probation Service. For some students the small voluntary organization may also be the only settings in which they will have opportunities to undertake certain types of work, such as with black service users, or working in partnership with people who have psychiatric illness. In this way a network placement can provide a student with direct work with service users in a non-statutory setting at the same time as statutory work elsewhere in the network, or with field work experience alongside having a role in the same agency as a group care worker. Through such experiences the student may 'hear the voice' of service users in the non-statutory or group care context in a way that their statutory setting and field work role might preclude. Yet the one experience may, through the process of reflection, immediately inform the other. Using Phillipson's (1992) model of perspective transformation (taken from the work of Mezirow, and from Freire) we can see that such an experience may result in students questioning and seeing afresh previously held beliefs about the 'proper' roles of social workers, and then going on to try out different options and so coming to new ways of seeing and acting.

Networks open up the likelihood of students encountering different styles of working, by virtue of the range of settings and numbers of professionals with whom they will come into contact. This was confirmed in our research, but was generally experienced as a help rather than as a hindrance. Encountering different styles of working has the potential to enhance a student's reflective practice. As Schön (1983) states 'the possible objects of his [sic] reflection are as varied as the kinds of phenomena before him and the systems of knowing-in-practice which he brings to them' (p. 62). Students in networks encounter more 'kinds of phenomena', and also divergent experiences of application of knowing-in-practice in different elements of the network. Experiencing different ways of making sense of problems, of interpreting legislation, or of working with users (to name a few) can facilitate their reflection on practice in the context of supervision. In his work on reflective practitioners Schön (1983, p. 61) comments on the benefits of such reflection, potentially serving as a 'corrective to over-learning'. He states 'through reflection, he [sic] can surface and criticize the tacit understandings that have grown up around repetitive experiences of a specialized practice, and can make a new sense of situations of uncertainty or uniqueness which he may allow himself to experience'. Situations of 'uncertainty and uniqueness' are commonly experienced by all students early in their placements, but for those in networks they are likely to feature throughout, as students are exposed to the range of learning opportunities, including these varied ways of working.

In addition to reflecting *on* practice (for example, in the context of supervision), Schön's model of the reflective practitioner identified the part played by 'reflection-in-action'. He suggests reflection-in-action is 'central to the art through which practitioners sometimes cope with the troublesome 'divergent' situations of practice' (1983, p. 62). As we have shown, students on network placements report experiencing plenty of 'divergent' situations in practice, some of which are experiences of divergence of practice by professionals. Such experiences can make an important contribution to their reflection-in-action; potentially prompting such thoughts as 'This is not working. Elsewhere (in the network) this would be approached differently. Can I try that approach here? Now?' Successful transfer of learning can therefore be viewed as evidence of a student's development as a reflective practitioner. Transfer of learning is more than crude transplanting of skills, requiring reflection on the sameness and the uniqueness of situations, and appropriate application in the light of these factors. Transfer of learning is also part of the process of reflection-in-action. As Papell and Skolnik (1992) write, 'Research, theory building, knowledge application, and skill refinement . . . are potentially contemporaneous elements in the reflection-in-action model' (p. 20).

In conclusion, network placements have much to offer students. With the enhanced learning opportunities, and with practice teachers who are inevitably at arm's length from at least part of the network, students are in a position to develop their abilities as reflective practitioners. What does our research tell us about setting up successful network placements? We identified key steps in the process that maximized the positive features of such placements whilst minimizing the potential drawbacks. In summary, the process should start with careful preparation of the student, and preparatory work with the component parts of the network placement, including identification of a network placement coordinator. Pre-placement planning meetings can follow the established pattern for singleton placements, but more time should be allowed. Lines of responsibility for the student's work, for supervision and practice teaching, and for gathering of evidence should be clarified. Does the student know who has the responsibility to make the final recommendation that they pass or fail the network placement? If these steps are followed, and expectations and responsibilities of all parties are clarified then network placements can take their place as an important element in a strategy for enhancing opportunities for students to develop as reflective practitioners.

References

Boutland K. and Baldwin M. (1991), *Only Connect: Placement Development between Voluntary and Statutory Agencies in the Fields of Child Protection and People with a Psychiatric History*. Bath: Bath University Practice Learning Centre.
Boutland K. and Batchelor J. (1993), *The Patterns that Connect: Action Research into Models of Network Placements for Social Work Students*. Bath: Bath University Practice Learning Centre.

Central Council for Education and Training in Social Work (1991), *Paper 30: Rules and Requirements for the Diploma in Social Work*, 2nd edn. London: CCETSW.

Day C. (1993), 'Reflection: A Necessary but not Sufficient Condition for Professional Development', *British Educational Research Journal*, **19** (1), 83–93.

Papell C. and Skolnik L. (1992), 'The Reflective Practitioner: A Contemporary Paradigm's Relevance for Social Work Education', *Journal of Social Work Education*, **28** (1), 18–26.

Phillipson J. (1992), *Practising Equality: Women, Men and Social Work*. London: CCETSW.

Pietroni M. (1995), 'The nature and aims of professional education for social workers', in M. Yelloly and M. Henkel (eds), *Learning and Teaching in Social Work: Towards Reflective Practice*. London: Jessica Kingsley Publishers.

Schön D. (1983), *The Reflective Practitioner*. New York: Basic Books.

Valli L. (1993), 'Reflective teacher education programs: an analysis of case studies', in James Calderhead and P. Gates (eds), *Conceptualizing Reflection in Teacher Development*. London: Falmer Press.

Webber R. (1992–1993), 'Developing Practice Placements in Community Care for Social Work Students', *Practice*, **6** (1), 70–78.

9 Managing for reflective learning

Phyllida Parsloe

Introduction

I have now had over twenty years of what, in 1995, I am prepared to describe as academic management although, in 1973, when I first became responsible for a university academic department, the word management would not have entered my mind as appropriate to describe even part of my job. However, times have changed and there is now no doubt that pro vice chancellors, deans, heads of departments and wardens of university halls of residence (all roles I have held or now fill) are managers. But what can they manage and what are appropriate ways of managing?

In speculating about these questions I shall draw mainly on my experience as a member and for over twelve years Head of the Social Work Department at the University of Bristol. During that period the staff group decided that the traditional approach to the education of social workers had to change. The traditional approach did not appear to prepare students adequately for the realities of the job, students became bored with the programme and did not bring into it their wide range of previous knowledge and experience, and its structure could not accommodate the ever increasing amount of knowledge social workers were expected to acquire. Faced with these facts the staff group decided to change to a programme based on self-directed, problem-based learning which would take place largely in small groups. The programme we developed we have called Enquiry and Action Learning (EAL) and it is described elsewhere in this book (Chapter 7).

The role of academic managers

To return to the first question; what can academic managers manage? It seems clear that despite what some try to do, what they can do is to manage some, but only some, aspects of the work and work environment of their peers. In this respect they resemble managers in any other organization whose job consists, in some part, of the management of professional colleagues. So they are like head teachers who manage fellow teachers, social service officers who manage social workers, and doctors who manage other doctors. They can manage those aspects of their colleagues' work for which the organization can be said to be accountable; the resources they need, their accommodation, their remuneration, promotion and conditions of work. What they cannot manage is the way in which their colleagues carry out the professional parts of their work. For example, management is not an activity which can be applied to how and what university colleagues teach, to their ideas for research, or to the way they write. Such activities can be influenced and shaped by peer discussion, encouraged by recognition, or stimulated by criticism, but they are ultimately not answerable to the level of control which a manager can exercise. Control stifles ideas and routinizes practice, as is all too clearly illustrated by some of the social work which is now carried out by overworked and overmanaged front-line staff in social services departments. Professionals must feel that their first and paramount responsibility is to those they serve, their students, clients or patients, to themselves and to their professional peers. This responsibility must take precedence over their accountability to the organization for which they work. I am not arguing for individual professional anarchy but for a recognition of the dual nature of the role of many employed people, especially those who work in the service industries. They are essentially bureau professionals and the challenge for them, and for those who are managers in service organizations, is to recognize the two aspects of the job and frame the appropriate structures and organization to support both. And these structures are not the same for the two types of activity.

Bureaucratic accountability is associated with a hierarchical organizational structure. Obviously it is a useful structure when the type of activity involved is the kind in which it makes sense for one person to be accountable to another and where people higher in the hierarchy can be expected to have the skills and knowledge to know whether those accountable to them are meeting the requirements of their jobs. Some aspects of the work of an academic fit this model, as do some parts of work of a social worker, school teacher or doctor. But for many parts of a professional's work, this is not the case. As an academic manager I work with colleagues, some of whom are intellectually much more able than I am, who are knowledgeable in areas about which I know virtually nothing and have teaching skills I do not possess. It would make no sense for them to be accountable to me for their thinking or their knowledge since I am less capable than they of judging these aspects of their work. The danger, however, is that hierarchical structures invade professional areas and when this happens professional standards are likely to fall and, in addition, management will lose credibility even in those areas which can and should be managed.

While I am clear that I cannot manage some aspects of my colleagues' work, my description may have suggested that a university head of department is only responsible for those aspects of the department which can be managed. This, of course, is one model for the management of professionals and is the one chosen by many of the hospital trusts who have appointed non-medical managers to clinical departments and made them responsible only for non-clinical activities, with consultants taking clinical responsibility. The alternative is to appoint, as head of department, someone to provide professional leadership and also to be a manager. This is the pattern in some hospitals, social services departments and universities, and, so far as I am aware, in all schools in the United Kingdom. In a university context, this means that the head of department, who traditionally has been a professor, will be a good enough academic to earn the respect of his or her peers, will have the leadership skills necessary to create a stimulating and critical peer culture and also the ability to manage those areas of departmental life which require management.

This may sound as if for some aspects of work, life in an academic department has a traditional hierarchical structure and so it does. The structure may differ slightly according to the area, for example, people may hold positions at a different level in financial matters than in those concerned with space (Figure 1).

Space hierarchy	Finance hierarchy
Vice Chancellor	Vice Chancellor
Bursar	Finance Director
Head of Department	Head of Department
Chair of Accommodation Committee	Department Finance Officer
All staff	All staff

Figure 1

For other parts of the work the structures are less clear and may consist of peer groupings. In the way I have described it, the two parts of work life, bureaucratic and professional, do not interact. This is obviously not the reality and yet it is difficult to describe or to illustrate diagrammatically. I found that Hampden-Turner and Trompenaars' (1994) account, of what they call Japanese puzzle box hierarchies, came nearer to my own experience (Figure 2).

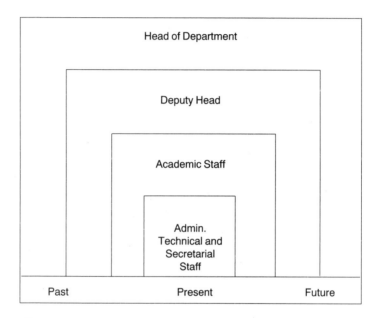

Figure 2
Source: Adapted from Hampden-Turner and Trompenaars (1994)

Instead of separate levels in a hierarchy, in this structure each higher level encompasses the one beneath it and the leader manager has his/her feet on the ground and is in touch with all levels of employees. This may be a truer representation of academic departments, where the heads do undertake some of the same work of teaching and research as does the newest academic recruit, than of Japanese industry where, I suspect, the boss does not actually work on the factory floor.

However, this foundation still imposes too much order on the messy reality of a typical academic department and obscures the fact that while the shape of the department may be relatively stable, the people occupying different roles change as managerial responsibilities are reallocated. The structure may be more like Figure 3.

Here the head of department and deputy have general responsibilities for

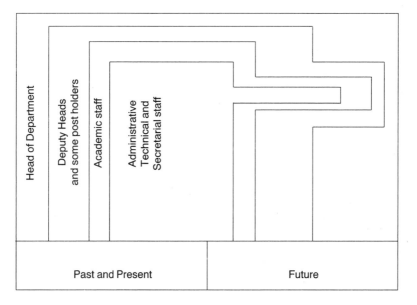

Figure 3

all management areas of the department's work and all other staff (or some other staff) carry responsibility for managing specific areas of the department's work, for example selection of students, assessment, finance or year convenorships. All contribute to policy formation and all to research and teaching.

This departmental organization is then part of the wider university system which has a similar mixture of management and academic concerns, although, at least as seen from below, the emphasis seems to be placed increasingly upon the managerial aspects

While I was preparing to write this article, I came across and re-read my old 1961 copy of the *Management of Innovation*. This book has just been re-issued with a new preface by Professor Tom Burns (Burns and Stalker 1994) and, as Lorenz (1994) says, in his review of the new edition, it is now clear how the concepts, which Burns and Stalker developed, have, insidiously, and without that source being recognized, influenced western management practice. Burns and Stalker rejected any mechanistic approach to leadership and management. They based their ideas upon a belief that human beings, given the right conditions, will motivate themselves and actively bring about changes and that the aim of organizations should be to create networks not hierarchies.

Leading and managing Enquiry and Action Learning

This approach to leadership and management is congruent with the intentions of social workers to value each individual, recognizing the unique contribution of each and to strive towards partnership and participation. I suspect that I have been greatly influenced by Burns and Stalker during the years in which the Bristol social work staff changed their teaching methods and tried to create a reflective learning environment for themselves and their students. I was not aware of this influence but I do know that I was persistently challenged by the question of the type of leadership and management that could best support both the change we were making and the particular kind of educational environment we hoped to create.

It was my belief that reflective learning could serve as a model for leadership and management but also that the leadership and management style had to be a model for reflective learning. In this way of thinking I relied heavily on Mattinson's (1992) idea of the reflection process. She argued that the style and nature of relationships between people at any level in the work of an organization will be repeated in other relationships at different levels. She based these ideas upon her experience of running a discussion group for probation officers. She found that when one of the officers described the work he or she was doing with a client, there was a tendency for the officer–client interactions to be repeated in the interactions between that officer and the group, but with the roles reversed. The officer seemed to take on the attitudes of the client and the group those of the officer. Mattinson argued that this provided a live opportunity to work on the problem of the officer–client interview because the same type of interaction was available in the discussion session. The logic of this is, of course, that human interactions have influence in all directions within an organization, providing models for good practice or setting up conflicts, competition and distrust. I am grateful to Janet Mattinson for these ideas, which have had a profound influence on me and convinced me that no interactions can take place within an organization without their ripples moving outwards and affecting other relationships and activities. This is, I suppose, a type of systems thinking but that has traditionally had more effect upon the way social workers and social work educators practise and teach about clients, than upon their own behaviour in organizations.

The theory of the reflection process imposes upon leaders and managers the necessity to recognize the way in which their behaviour will, whether they like it or not, provide a model for practice. There are, however, other reasons to do so, which arise from the nature of social work and of education, and which are very important. They are concerned with change. It is the job of social work to help individuals, families and groups to find ways of altering their situations and/or themselves so that the social problems which they face can be solved or at least lived with more comfortably. Education is also about change in the way we see and understand the world and when the education is for professional practice it also involves change in the way we act and the way we use knowledge in interaction with other people. Managing an educational institution is therefore concerned with creating the conditions under which staff can assist students to change and this often means that staff too must change.

In moving from a social work programme, based at least in part upon a traditional view of the roles of students and of teachers, to an Enquiry and Action Learning (EAL) programme, we were aware that we were introducing a major change and that almost every aspect of our behaviour would have to change. We had some guiding principles which were drawn from research into adult learning. We believed, on the basis of this evidence, that adults learn best when they work in groups, on problems, using their past experience and when they control their own learning.

It seemed that these principles should be equally applicable to management and leadership of a department moving towards active learning and this has proved to be the case.

Working in groups on problems

We were fortunate that, as a department, we had a tradition of working in groups and even more fortunate that there were amongst us a number of very skilled group workers. We were also lucky that during the period in which we were changing our programme, we were still of a size which allowed us to handle all major policy discussions and decisions in our general monthly departmental meeting. The meetings were often long, the agenda overloaded and occasionally the atmosphere was tense, but this meeting was a major way by which information was shared and everyone was involved in the decision making. Attendance was remarkably high and it was an expectation that everyone came. This meeting often referred items for detailed work to smaller groups and the preparatory work of the department was carried on in groups, usually of between three and five people. This was what the department wanted and, although there were many occasions when I would have much preferred to see some work done by one person, this very seldom happened. Looking back, I think it was a strength rather than the waste of staff time which I sometimes thought.

Establishing a new style of teaching based largely upon student groups with staff facilitators required a much more collective approach than does the traditional single person lecture course. So, not only in policy making but also in learning the new role of facilitator rather than information giving teachers, staff worked in groups. And in all groups staff worked on problems although I use the word not in a negative sense but to convey the idea that the task of the group was to develop an answer to some teaching or administrative question and to do so in a way that was congruent with the principles of EAL.

Another factor which helped us to change was the size of the staff group. For most of the period of change we consisted of about fourteen people and this may be an ideal sized group for change through consensus. I came to Bristol from a much smaller university department where I had five colleagues and I look back upon this previous job with considerable guilt and distress. Six is a very difficult number, especially when it includes, as my staff group did, one senior and powerful man and one woman (myself) of the same kind. We behaved like a family with warring parents and had great difficulty escaping from this dynamic which seemed to engage the more primitive parts of our personalities. I do not know whether all such small organizational groups run the risk of replicating unhelpful family dynamics. I do know, however, that when I came to Bristol, to a larger staff group, I was able to use the more adult parts of my personality and, as a result, to develop, grow and change. I believe strongly that work organizations should avoid aping family structures and dynamics if they wish to engage the most adult parts of their staff in the work to be done.

This belief has influenced my behaviour as a manager since one of the things to which I have given conscious attention is how to ensure that both staff and students are treated as responsible adults. This has meant that we have developed a culture, certainly amongst staff, of having high expectations of each other. We assume people will do what they say they will do, will meet deadlines and contain themselves. I am not altogether sure we always create the same expectation of students, although EAL is built upon the premise that students are self-directing, responsible adults and by and large they more than prove that this is the case. There is always, however, a temptation for both students and staff to slip back into a relationship in which the teacher takes inappropriate control. One of the roles of head of department is to help the staff group resist the pressures they and the students create towards too much rule making, clarification and rigidity. Holding the tension between chaos and rigidity, and knowing which is appropriate where, are important tasks for academic managers in an active learning programme.

Using past experience

Using past experience was part of the problem-solving process we were helping students to acquire. I am not sure, however, the extent to which we articulated it in our own processes of change but past experience was of course always present. Often we used it as a guide to what we did not want to do again; we were very consciously changing because of the identified weaknesses of past practice.

We were, I think, fortunate that we did not experience many staff changes during the five years leading up to the implementation of EAL. So we had a shared history and the only person who joined us was appointed to research the change and was selected for her commitment to the type of education we were creating. I suspect we would have found it difficult to incorporate new staff at this time and to value the experiences they brought. Since implementing EAL we have had a series of staff changes as some of our senior and experienced staff left to take up professorships and, like any established group, we have not found it entirely easy to involve newcomers, especially when they questioned our new creation. We developed a buddy system for new colleagues, whom we paired with an existing staff member, which seemed to help the entry problems and allow the existing group to value the new experiences brought by the newcomers. But there were still difficulties in entering a system which depended largely on consensus decision making and felt more chaotic than managed.

Control

Control of the many aspects of the change was shared amongst the staff group. However, two staff took on the major planning and development work but with policy decisions always coming back to the general meeting. For part of the development period I was head of department and I put a considerable amount of thought into the ways in which I should and would use the authority attached to that role. In Bristol University, at that time, the head of a department had vague but extensive powers. Some staff had contracts which included the clause that they should do what was required by the head of department. Bristol was a departmental university and the heads were often referred to collectively as the barons. Apart from me, they were all men.

I chaired the departmental meetings, not entirely because I wanted to but because I never managed to get an alternative system agreed. In them I tried to be sure that I did not attempt to manage the areas of my colleagues' lives which I considered to be those which depended upon their professional judgement and skills and I tried to ensure that no other individuals or groups did so either. Within the areas which could be managed and for which the university could hold me accountable, my policy was to make clear, in departmental meetings, when the meeting was free to make the decision and when I was, in effect, seeking advice on which I would base the decision I would take. My own view, although my colleagues may not share it, is that there were few areas where decisions were not delegated to the group and these mostly concerned individual staff. In large part this was because the staff group had developed ways of reaching a consensus and I was very seldom required to decide between conflicting views. The staff group was, and still is, highly collaborative and my experience has convinced me that if one waits, unexpected solutions often emerge from what appear to be widely divided views. This means that everyone has to be able to stand a considerable degree of confusion, sometimes for a long while. Here, our backgrounds as social workers and social scientists stood us in good stead. We were all aware of the importance of process and were prepared to spend time on it. I realized, if I did not know it before, when I moved into the wider university arena, that this is not universal and that many people are extremely impatient of time spent on the process of decision making and cannot tolerate the confusion. They press for quick decisions and have no doubt that the decision is all that matters. I wonder whether this is particularly true of scientists and engineers, perhaps because their training is for work with inhuman materials. I remember one of our Vice Chancellors, when he was cross with me that as Dean I had not yet got my faculty to reach some decision, telling me that it was the decision that was important and the process only mattered about one per cent. I argued for a much more even distribution of importance, not least because the process or means influences the decision in the end. We agreed to disagree. Waiting for consensus has, however, been an important part of developing EAL. It took us at least eight years to decide to change, select the way we wanted to change and then to plan and implement the change. At times, I, who am an impatient person, found it almost unbearably slow but I was convinced we could only move forward when everyone was prepared to do so. I also believed that, with our particular staff group, agreement was a realistic if long-term prospect and so it proved to be. It accounts for much of our successful change.

A just department

There was another consideration which influenced my management style and which does not fall within the guiding principles for adult learning, but does arise from the fact that our job as educators and the job of social workers demands we base what we do upon values about the proper way for people to treat fellow citizens. As a staff group, we shared strong views about the need for staff and students to respect and value each other and treat each other justly. It was of great importance that we ran the department in ways which were based upon ideas of natural justice so that students would have a model to use in future practice. We spent a great deal of time developing just procedures for assessment and for the handling of disputes and for separating decisions about standards from those concerned with mitigating circumstances. Having established a firm base here we have now moved on to the much more difficult area of anti-discriminatory practice and the creation of equal opportunities.

Managing workloads

During the years we were developing EAL there were some shifts in the university towards, if not greater democracy, at least a greater requirement that staff should be consulted about major decisions. It also became accepted, largely, I suspect, because of the increasing range of duties being imposed upon heads of departments, that they would delegate some of these tasks to academic colleagues. In the Social Work Department there had always been a degree of delegation but this increased as the department enlarged and diversified. In 1979 when the department was created, it did no more than run two programmes; a one-year course for social science graduates and a two-year course for non-graduates. Staff did virtually no research, although they did publish in social work journals and occasionally ran conferences and short courses. The situation now is quite different. Department staff are all engaged in some research, often outside funded, and they therefore buy themselves out of some teaching. This allows us to bring in experienced practitioners to join the teaching team. We now offer an undergraduate degree, several taught Masters programmes, and have a large number of students registered for a PhD or MPhil by research. These changes would be significant without also redesigning the DipSW programme.

The changes were led by staff and increasingly staff took on responsibility for sections of the department's work. I have always been slightly unhappy with the idea that their managerial authority was delegated. Staff remained accountable to faculty, senate and council for the way they used their delegated authority but their accountability was not direct; it ran through the head of department. Most of the time this goes unnoticed. It is when things go wrong that it becomes apparent. Here I had to discover, and for me quite painfully, my own weaknesses. What I have learned is that I cope easily with things going wrong provided I am warned about them in advance. Often it is easy to find ways to solve the problem or limit the damage so long as one is not the person at the centre of the difficulty. One of the most satisfying parts of my job as a manager is the power, on occasions, to put things right. But the reverse side of that is that I find it hard to tolerate situations which blow up, so to speak, in my face and when the first I know about them is on some public occasion. Over the years I have learned which of my colleagues have an eye for the situations which might blow up and which either have no such sense or, if they have, react by keeping it to themselves.

The way in which we allocate management roles in the department has traditionally been by a rather unstructured system of bids, offers and persuasion culminating in a departmental meeting at which we check that all tasks are covered for the coming year and find ways of filling any gaps. This has never been an easy process and it is becoming more difficult as the total workload increases, the university devolves more work to departments, and the expectations on staff to research and publish increase. Against this background, issues about equity in work allocation are more often raised and pressure has increased for a more transparent workload allocation system in which everyone carries a similar load.

I have always had difficulty with this concept of equality. My colleagues are very able people and I am extremely fortunate that I have none whom I would prefer not to have in the department. But they are very different from each other and the differences are not just in areas of expertise but also in the speed at which they work and the level of stress they can accommodate. The pressure towards equal loads ignores such human differences and also seems to me to conflict with a genuine notion of equal opportunities. It is, of course, compounded in a system, like the universities, where there are no fixed hours of work or nationally agreed ways of defining work patterns. I am not arguing for the introduction of a working week since academic staff might lose more than they would gain and the loss would be to the professional autonomy which in many universities they still have in large measure.

But the problem of workloads remains and is the one most likely to cause dissent in our usually collaborative department. The department meeting decided to set up a system of points for different teaching and administrative tasks and our work towards workload scores has been helpful, although it is not yet complete. This gives an allocation of hours for each task and whether a particular staff member takes more or less time than the allocation is ignored. There is a natural tendency for staff to press for every bit of work they undertake to be built into the system. This could lead to a rigidity which would damage cooperation and initiatives although this has not been apparent yet. We hope it may be possible to prove that a collaborative system of work allocation is possible and that it works in providing a good quality learning environment of students and staff. In the current climate of individual financial targets or minimum required face-to-face teaching hours, a more collegiate alternative is certainly needed.

In addition to the question of equity in teaching loads, there is also the knotty question of how workloads are constructed. Some tasks are more popular than others; some convey more status and some are more likely, it is thought, to enhance the prospects of promotion. An area of work which is always problematical in academic social work departments is the organization of practice placements for students. Despite the fact that DipSW programmes are run by a partnership of the university and social welfare agencies, changes in the field mean that placements are increasingly hard to find and a very large amount of the time of staff in the partnership is spent here. Recently, and for the first time, my colleagues and I had a major disagreement about the way in which I handled the allocation of the task of Placement Coordination. Normally this would be arranged by formal and informal negotiations. On this occasion these seemed to have failed and, when we were apparently deadlocked in a departmental meeting, I decided to announce the names of the three people whom, if need be, I would require to share this task. It was a serious mistake on my part since I was behaving outside my usual style and in a way which undermined the self-directed management which is essential to a programme offering self-directed learning to its students. I should have waited, stood a bit more uncertainty, and trusted my colleagues. Now we have to rebuild collaboration and it takes much longer to create than it does to destroy.

The university and the world of social work

So far I have concentrated on the way the staff group worked together to create Enquiry and Action Learning and to some aspects of my role as head of department in this. What I have not addressed is the way in which we worked within the wider university and the social work world in order to introduce a learning programme which was new to both.

As a manager I had the great advantage that Bristol was my second professorial appointment and I could therefore move into a new department leaving behind some of the mistakes I made the first time round. I was also in a position to know some of the choices that needed to be made. In my first head of department post I had acted in such a way that I developed the standing of the department externally amongst government departments and social work agencies to a considerable extent by taking a high profile myself in the Scottish welfare and criminal justice scene. This meant that I probably paid too little attention to the position of the department in the university. I also realize that I was escaping some of the 'family' conflicts in the department by being away quite a lot of the week.

When I moved to Bristol I came to a department already quite well known nationally. It was also in England, where the opportunities open to social work professors to engage in national activities are far more limited than they are in Scotland. In England the pond is larger and the professional social work fish more plentiful. My job in Bristol was to develop the newly created Social Work Department which brought together two parts of the university in which social work programmes had formerly been offered. I decided that the most important task was to ensure that as a department we had a secure place in the university and that we were well known there.

At first some of my colleagues, especially those who came from what was then the Extra Mural Department, found it difficult to feel part of the university, but this gradually changed and they and I moved into roles within the Faculty and the wider university. We had a lot to offer, not least an understanding of process. This widening of contacts stood us in good stead when it came to introducing our new DipSW to the Faculty and obtaining consent for it. We had two points in our favour in addition to the, to us, undoubted merits of our programme. Many of us were known personally to our faculty colleagues and secondly social work was, to put it mildly, not considered academically important. The latter may explain why, in a very traditional faculty, we were able to introduce an innovative programme which contained no unseen examinations. That, I believe, would have been impossible in any of the basic social science disciplines at that time or if we were running an undergraduate or a Masters programme. A diploma did not need to raise such concerns about academic standards. Later, when we changed in part to a Masters programme, the climate had changed too.

Managing a social work department means looking beyond the university to agency partners and to the validating body for social work, the Central Council for Education and Training in Social Work (CCETSW). There has always been tension between agencies and social work courses and the new partnership arrangements introduced by CCETSW were intended to alleviate these. To some extent they have done so and in Bristol we have been very fortunate in our partners. However, serious problems remain and they are compounded by the organizational changes and financial cuts taking place in both sectors. The major difficulty, I believe, is the ambivalent attitude which social welfare agencies, along with the general public, hold towards education for social work. There is a persistent belief amongst some managers, especially in local authority social services departments, that social workers need training, not education, and that social work courses in universities unfit people for the job they have to do. This is the agency version of the public view that anyone can do social work and all that is required is common-sense. In many social services departments there is a profoundly anti-intellectual climate. This is not true of the people who serve on the committees of the DipSW partnership but they tend to be people who are in training roles within their agencies and who are, to an extent, marginalized themselves. What is difficult is to get on to these committees agency staff who actually have the same authority to commit resources as do the university staff. The head of department is always the university co-chair of the DipSW programme management group. The agency co-chairs, both very able women, have been in the local authority training department and without line management authority. Senior local authority managers do not serve on DipSW management groups and why should they? Social work education is a very small part of their many and pressing concerns.

A book could be written about what I see as the myth of DipSW partnership and their management problems; here all I want to do is to draw attention to the difficulties and to the amount of agency and academic time and good will which goes into attempting to operate an essentially flawed system. In Bristol we were, however, fortunate in that our partners supported our move to EAL and some played a major role in informing their agencies about it.

Major changes such as we were making have also to obtain the approval of CCETSW since, without their validation, the programme would not qualify students for professional practice. Here again, personal relationships and status eased our path. We involved the CCETSW staff member who was our adviser from the start and found ready support from him. In the social work world our status was the reverse of what it was in the university. We are a relatively large programme with a good reputation and members of our staff have held major roles in the various national and international social work organizations as well as within the Council itself. We never needed to take on the Council about the changes we were making but we could have and would have had it been necessary. And had we needed to, our very good links with the university Law Department might have been called in aid.

Writing this final section has made me question my own approach. I enjoy managing but I get different kinds of satisfaction from different parts of my job. Sometimes, as is often the case with CCETSW and sometimes with the University, it has the attributes of a complicated game which challenges me intellectually but, unless ethical issues are involved, not emotionally. The day-to-day management of the department is emotionally rewarding and can be very stressful because it concerns the lives of people I care about and whose liking and respect I want and want to keep. With staff and students there is no element of a game; it is for real.

References

Burns, T. and Stalker, G.M. (1994), *The Management of Innovation*, 3rd edn. Oxford: Oxford University Press.

Hampden-Turner, C. and Trompenaars, F. (1994), *The Seven Cultures of Capitalism*. London: Piatkus.

Lorenz, C. (1994), *Financial Times*, 28 November.

Mattinson, J. (1992), *The Reflection Process in Casework Supervision*. London: Tavistock Institute of Medical Psychology.

10 Team and management consultation: reflections on the world's third oldest profession

Brian Dimmock

The very highest is barely known by men.
Then comes that which they know and love,
Then that which is feared,
Then that which is despised.

He who does not trust enough will not be trusted.
When actions are performed

Without unnecessary speech,
People say, 'We did it!'

Lao Tsu, Tao Te Ching (sixth century BC)

Introduction

This chapter is about team and management development and consultation in human service organizations. It will attempt to demystify the terms 'development' and 'consultation' which are somewhat overloaded with either scepticism or magical powers. In the Old Testament of the Bible, Joseph advised the Pharaoh about his dreams; was he using a 'reflective' rather than 'expert' approach? A more recent popular exponent of the art, Sir John Harvey Jones, has ably demonstrated the 'expert' approach in the popular British television series called 'The Trouble-shooter' and in the book of the same name (Harvey Jones 1990). His pedigree for such a role is unquestionable, as he was for many years the managing director of one of the world's major multinational companies, Imperial Chemical Industries (ICI). Schön (1983) characterizes 'expert' professional practice as, '. . . instrumental problem solving made rigorous by the application of scientific theory and technique'.

In contrast, he sees the 'reflective' practitioner as being able to proceed in situations of uncertainty precisely because he is not '. . . bound by technical rationality'. Thus, unlike the familiar process model of diagnosis and treatment, or assessment and intervention, the reflective approach does not separate thinking from doing, but combines them in creating a '. . . theory of the unique case'.

This chapter will also provide the reader with a chance to consider the difference between 'expert' and 'reflective' approaches and ask whether one is better than the other, or whether it is a question of 'horses for courses'. Would Sir John have been able to help the Pharaoh by advising him to move out of grain production and into the chocolate locust business? Would Joseph have asked the Managing Director of the Norton Motorcycle Company, a famous but ailing British business, to recall his most recent dream? The Norton is, after all, reputed by biking aficionados to be a 'dream machine'.

A common complaint about 'expert' management consultancy is that it is strong on diagnosing the problem and even proposing a solution, but weak on helping people to turn this into a reality. On the other hand, the 'reflective' approach is vulnerable to complaints that it may merely 'reflect' the obvious, i.e. tell everyone what they already know. Indeed, one popular definition of a consultant is 'someone who steals your watch to tell you the time'! When applied to the human service organizations, the 'expert' approach relies on seeing problems as of a technical nature in a service whose ideology stresses the personal, and the importance of human communication and relationships.

With the introduction of market principles drawn from business practice into this sector, in the health service and other social welfare organizations, is the reflective approach, with all its respect for human diversity and ideology of empowerment, going to survive the creeping tide of managerialism (Strong and Robinson 1988; Walker 1992)? Or will it be recognized as a necessary antidote to the epidemic of stress and burn out which appear to inflict human service organizations (see, for example Fineman 1985; Ross and Seeger 1988; Yancik 1984)? Will it help to stem the tide of managerialism, or will consultants just be used to help staff adjust to a less caring and 'person-centred' culture?

In the spirit of our post-modern age, the readers must decide these issues for themselves knowing the bias of the author. By describing work which uses a particular approach to 'reflective practice' it is to commend it to others as being both helpful and empowering to individuals. It challenges staff and the organization of which they are a part. It recognizes imbalances of power and seeks a pragmatic way forward without ducking moral, political and spiritual issues. It encourages such questions as: where am I in this dilemma? what resources do I have at my disposal to influence events? how do my actions affect others? do I have control, influence, or just hope in this situation? It is based on the belief that human beings have to know and tell their story of events and discover what they mean and have them heard by others; that human beings are scientists and like to experiment and can be enormously creative; and that the enemy of such creativity is fear, extreme vulnerability and ambition for its own sake.

Our version of the reflecting team

The model we have used in our work with teams is largely based on the work of family therapists of the 'constructivist' school (Hoffman 1988; Anderson and Goolishian 1988; Andersen 1987), and the summary below is adapted from the work of Robinson (1991). Anderson and Goolishian describe therapy as 'the development through dialogue, of new themes and narratives, and actually the creation of new histories'.

This builds on the tradition in psychotherapy derived from Freud's analytical approach to the past of his patients. The difference is that the 'interpretation' of the past is not mediated solely by the expert, but constructed through a partnership of therapist and client. Freud was working within the paradigm of medicine with its tradition of what Schön (1983) calls 'expert knowledge'. By contrast, practitioners such as Hoffman (1988) are drawing on 'reflective knowledge', which is about the creation of knowledge by engaging in a unique process with the client.

In this approach, careful attention is given to language which defines social organization. For example, in one organization which provides services for children who have been abused, some staff said that they had been abused by their manager. By coining this phrase it defines the organizational structure through an analogy with abusive parent–child relationships despite the fact that all staff are adults. This was echoed in the descriptions by managers of some of their teams, who saw their staff as behaving like 'adolescents'. This reflected a different perspective on the parent–child analogy, where parents often feel less influential or able to control their adolescent children. The same type of language was used to construct very different meaning systems about relationships between managers and team members. In the case of the former, managers were constructed as abusive adults; in the latter, managers saw themselves as struggling to control rebellious adolescents.

In another organization which worked with people who have been imprisoned for their beliefs, staff expressed the view that they 'felt like prisoners' of the organization, on this occasion, constructing a 'story' of the organization which parallels the gaoler and the gaoled. We go full circle by linking Hoffman's (1988) belief that client and therapist might develop a shared unconscious which can be approached through stories, trance or dreams. Perhaps Joseph could have used his consultation techniques with the Norton Motorcycle Company after all!

It is tempting to see such use of language as merely a reflection of the way an organization is structured which is bound to be described by familiar words and concepts, particularly at a time of stress and conflict. However, the constructivists go further by arguing that social systems, such as organizations, do not create problems; rather it is problems which define a system; this system may then come to represent the organization for any individual or group within it at a particular time, or in relation to particular aspects of organizational relationships.

Such an approach to language and meaning is antithetical to expert knowledge, because if, as consultants, we participate in helping others to construct meaning, we cannot stand outside the process as 'objective'. This 'expert' style is adopted by Sir John Harvey Jones (1990). He starts off his consultations by engaging in a dialogue with his clients, although very much one which he appears to dominate. His reputation as an expert may overwhelm some of the participants who often appear as if they are 'sitting at the feet' of a prophet. The TV programmes finish with him delivering his advice in a firm, kindly and engaging style reminiscent of an old-fashioned family doctor. This advice might include fairly extreme measures, such as sacking the sales manager and stopping production of their best selling line. The solution always appears to be logical because by force of personality and the authority of his reputation, he tries to impose his own 'story' on the problems of the firm in question. Some politicians are expert at this type of attempt to impose meaning on events. Former British prime minister, Mrs Thatcher's acronym of TINA (there is no alternative) is a classic example.

In contrast to Sir John Harvey Jones' (1990) approach which seeks to find allies in an organization for his understanding of the problems, a reflective practitioner tries to hold on to several different understandings of the problem simultaneously. This enables the participants to start to enquire about other views, or create new ones which emerge out of the dialogue. The team or group then attempts to create mutual stories which take account of differences, conflicts and new possibilities.

We must be careful to stress that the reflective approach does not negate hierarchy. Rather, it seeks to differentiate it. For example, if you ask a group of children who is the biggest a consensus will probably emerge and a tall/fat child will be pushed forward. If, on the other hand, you explore what biggest means to them all you may arrive at biggest feet, biggest appetite, biggest eyes, biggest heart! The approach de-emphasizes hierarchy by clarifying distinctions. In some work with a group of women who ran a service for other women, it was apparent to the consultant that there were many conflicts within the group which could not emerge because of a group ideology which emphasized that women were cooperative, non-competitive, and consensus seeking. When taking into account that the organization was helping to deal with the consequences of male violence, this ideology repre-

sented many useful truths for those involved. Unfortunately, it also pre-
vented the best use of the group's resources, as none of the group were willing to push themselves forward as a leader on any matter for fear of being
seen as acting like an aggressive male. A way round this was found by
exploring continuums of 'more or less' experience in a wide range of distinct
but overlapping areas. For example, more or less time as a volunteer, more or
less training in a particular area, more or less experience in face-to-face contact with clients. As each participant began to identify her own areas of
strength, it became easier to accept that a plurality of hierarchies existed
which then gave individuals permission to 'take the lead' without feeling
they were adopting 'masculine' behaviour.

It is also important to note that the consultant does not become a mere
cypher for the ideas of others; rather, she is a full participant who seeks to
develop her own ideas and repertoire of knowledge and beliefs. The reflective approach to consultation and team development requires that the consultants develop a dialogue between themselves and or with herself. This
includes a dialogue with her own beliefs, and that the *process* of this dialogue
is shared, not just a summary of the outcome which is then presented as
'expert' advice.

Finally, one of the criticisms of some of the earlier constructivist
approaches to therapy (Hoffman 1990) was that power differences between
participants, including the therapist, and between the problem system and
other systems, were ignored or negated. Again, Sir John's approach encapsu-
lates a view which seeks to mobilize support for a particular definition of a
problem, and then to use any 'legitimate' means to impose it on others. The
participants are sorted into those who can accept 'the necessary changes' and
those who cannot. In a reflective approach to consultation, the emphasis is
on the reciprocal nature of power. It has to acknowledge that this reciprocity
operates within wider belief systems about how power is distributed which
will limit the extent to which any given group can operationalize their newly
created beliefs about their problems or potential.

Given that the emphasis in the reflective model is on the process by which
knowledge and meaning are created between people through dialogue
(although it does incorporate the notion of dialogues within the self), we
have found that a reflecting 'team' approach to management and team consultation provides increased scope to demonstrate reflection. It also escapes
the restrictions of the 'expert' model whereby the consultant has to come up
with ideas and 'sell' them to the team. This is drawn from the work of therapists such as Andersen (1987) who provide consultation for families by
members of the therapeutic team commenting spontaneously on what they
think is happening and then engaging in a dialogue with family members
about the utility of these thoughts. We have adapted this approach to team
consultation and development. Typically, we will ask those taking part in

the team development or consultation exercise to discuss issues which have been identified by them as germane to their problems or needs. We will then discuss our ideas about their conversation, with each other and with them. Sometimes we will structure this quite formally; we discuss it, they comment on our discussion, we react to their comments. At other times, we will engage directly in conversation with them and then try and get agreement on the themes and issues which emerge. Our 'expertise' is in facilitating this process, theirs is in their circumstances and their work. The following summary of two different contexts in which the approach is used is drawn from our practice as team/management consultants.

Two contexts for applying the reflecting team approach

Pioneers of the application of systems theory to therapeutic work with families (Minuchin 1974; Haley 1987) were quick to identify the referral stage of the process of work with families as critical. Haley, in particular, developed a set of questions which included assessing the 'position' of each participant on the problem. Going a step further, the struggle to define the problem in a particular way was also seen as crucial to the outcome. 'Reframing' the problem was a technique which was quickly established by family therapists as part of their repertoire (Watzlawick, Weakland and Fisch 1974). Pioneers in this style of work such as Minuchin (1974) were later criticized as adopting an 'expert' style of reframing which imposed his own ideas on the family members. Minuchin was one of the first therapists to include the 'referrer' in his family interviews, suggesting that the way in which organizations impact on individuals becomes part of the way in which problems are defined, and are maintained. Such an approach also developed through 'network therapy' (Dimmock and Dungworth 1985) in an attempt to widen the context in which problems have their meaning, and to expand the opportunities for creating new 'stories' about the people involved.

The consultation style we have developed from using the reflecting team approach involves focusing on the 'stories' which emerge from whichever group is convened. As team and management consultants we could rely on the status of being 'experts' and then attempt to use the power this gives us to impose demands on who takes part, and to diagnose the problem and propose a cure. However, we prefer to accept that ultimately we are relatively powerless in the face of a complex organization with its own unique and complex history. Our approach is to offer to listen to whoever wishes to take part in an initial meeting to discuss how we might be of help. Our role is to listen and to give some immediate feedback to those taking part in the form of a dialogue with them and between ourselves, with the participants observing and commenting. From this initial process we then attempt to establish the focus for the work and how it will proceed. As far as possible we try to ensure that all negotiations about this process are conducted through the proper organizational structures.

The two contexts outlined below are to some extent 'ideal types', but in practice they overlap and we may combine work from each. They represent our 'story' of the experience we have had in this work and they are bound to differ from accounts that others who have taken part would give. The first is 'The troubled team in a time of change'; the second is 'Team development – it's not that we're not a good team it's just that we think we could be so much better'. Whichever of the two contexts are considered, the issues outlined above will apply.

The troubled team in a time of change

In the case of team consultation in personal social services work, managers often call in consultants when a team is seen as being in turmoil, conflict and disarray. In a sense, managers are saying that there is an element to the team's needs which can best be provided by outsiders, or that their own ability to help the team members through the problems they are facing is affected by their own role, perhaps because there are disciplinary proceedings going on, or because the problems have been such that a 'them and us' culture has developed around the boundary of managers and practitioners.

Bringing in consultants can be seen as a way for managers to avoid taking responsibility for problems, or trying to recruit allies. It may also be viewed as an attempt to 'pathologize' team members ('this team needs help, they've been through a lot'). There is also the possibility that it is a way for managers to avoid conflicts between themselves about what to do, or for some managers to recruit allies in their own struggle to define the problems in a particular way. Such negative connotations tend to rely on assumptions about the motivation of others, which is an inexact science at the best of times.

An example

In one case we were asked to help a child protection team (which included social workers, family care workers and administrators) who had been systematically bullied, harassed and intimidated by a team manager. After three years, some of the team members managed to get together and report his abuse to senior managers. Team members were in a varied state of anger and shock, with high rates of sickness and other signs of serious stress. They were at pains to point out that despite all this they had always been determined to maintain their high standards of work. At the time of the consultation, the team manager was suspended pending disciplinary action and investigation of the complaints. In the meantime, radical changes to the team's functions and jobs were being planned.

Having finally managed to act to deal with their manager, the team members who were instrumental in 'blowing the whistle' found that those not involved did not share their views entirely, or agree with their chosen way forward. They began to feel that managers felt that they were 'trouble-makers' and that their heroic efforts to keep the work going were not recognized. In addition, in order to do what they had done they had to develop the kind of solidarity which left little scope for recognizing their own differences and conflicts. A powerful analogy developed with the role of the abused child who reports the abuser and is then 'blamed' by others.

Our approach to this was to suggest that some time be spent together 'telling the story' of the events which led up to the 'whistle blowing'. As the story emerged it was apparent that there were several stories and versions of events – a collective version emerged, but each individual's story was also told and placed in relation to others. Similarities and differences emerged. Women were intimidated differently from men; social workers were threatened in different ways from administrators and family care workers; each individual's fear, and ultimately how they found inspiration to act courageously, were compared and contrasted. A subtle web of overlapping and conflicting motives emerged as the basis for the collective will to act. Instead of seeing themselves as a beleaguered band of survivors, the full story of the extent of the obstacles they faced and the effort needed to act created the opportunity to change the story. The differences between them were no longer seen as a threat to solidarity, but as a useful diversity. As their differences emerged, their 'threat' to others diminished, as they could be seen as individuals rather than a hostile collectivity.

In our view, attempting to present an 'expert' diagnosis of the problems encountered in these circumstances would have created powerful resonances with the style of the team manager, whose approach to his task was to ensure the survival of 'his' team in the face of encroaching change. He did this by seeking allies within the team and beyond, making and breaking temporary alliances and coalitions without fully sharing his own vision with others. There was a powerful identification between himself and the work of the team, and differences with his approach were seen as personal attacks on him. To prevent this he developed a controlling style which restricted the truth to his own version of events. An 'expert' approach to such a management problem might easily involve trying to sell a solution through seeking allies in much the same way as the team manager had gone about his task. Although it might be presented with a different personal style to the previous 'authoritarian' one, it would inevitably be identified with the consultant, rather than as the collective efforts of consultant and consultees.

It's not that we're not a good team, it's just that we think we could be so much better

The engagement of consultants to help with team development may be an attempt to recapture lost feelings from an earlier stage in the team's life, in some ways analogous with marital enrichment for couples who miss the enthusiasm and inventiveness of their earlier love-making. It can also be seen as a solution to a sense of bewilderment and confusion, or an attempt to take stock before, during or after change. Where are we? who are we? what are we? how do others see us? are the kinds of questions being asked. In our experience there are usually one or two enthusiasts within the team for this approach, and the others go along with it either through inertia, curiosity or a lack of desire to question the sense of the suggestion. Approaches to it vary from intensive group activities in wild countryside, to group dynamic exercises involving cushions, lengthy silences and emotional outbursts. Managers may see it as a reward for hard work, a way of easing in difficult changes, or the kind of indulgence which those who have had social work training appear to think is essential from time to time.

Our attitude to team development is that any sane organization which expects its staff to undertake difficult and stressful work will want its staff to take time out to think and reflect on what they are doing and how they can retain their enthusiasm and creativity. At its best and simplest it is time/space for each individual to tell their own story of the team, and for the 'team's' story to be updated and agreed. It is not akin to the kind of commercial or quasi-religious activity which is designed to increase the identification of the individual with the organization. If organizations become only a series of changing enthusiasms, then staff will always have the fear that their own current identification with the organization will easily be replaced with new enthusiasms which belong to others. This engenders obedience, not creativity.

The role of the reflective management consultant is again a facilitative one. It will allow time for the 'accepted' story of the team to be told, and for the differences and new versions to find space. Somehow, participants must be given the opportunity to say, 'I used to think that, but now I think this', or 'I'm more interested in this now, and although I know you all see me as an expert on that, I'm finding it hard to stay enthusiastic'. The consultant's job is to judge the pace at which participants wish to go, and to make them feel safe to try out new or controversial aspects of their own story of the team. It is helping the team to harness differences and conflict by giving them space to explore diversity.

An example

An opportunity arose for us to work with four different teams from within one organization. The organization was undergoing considerable change which was making an impact on teams in quite different ways. Changes in the focus of the work and in the management structure were all putting teams under pressure. Managers recognized that teams could benefit from time to build their new identities to face the challenging times ahead.

We offered to work with all the teams together, with scope to work with individual teams both during this joint work and in subsequent sessions if this was felt desirable. Our thoughts were that bringing the teams together might help to decrease isolation in that common issues would reduce the sense that 'there must be something wrong with us, I bet other teams don't have these problems'. It would also increase the range and diversity of experience, especially if we could help to find ways of making this available across teams. The problem was the numbers involved and our sense that we would find it difficult to help such a large group develop the degree of trust in each other and us to be able to make use of the opportunities.

Tempting as it was, we managed to avoid indulging in a series of exercises which would have been interesting, but no more than the sum of the parts of the different groups' experience. While sharing this dilemma with those attending, a solution emerged. We would demonstrate some of the simple techniques of reflective conversations, and then teams would act as reflective consultants for each other, with us observing and offering a further 'layer' of reflection to the pairs of teams and the group overall.

By trusting in the ability of the consultation process we were able to avoid 'applying' exercises and models of 'team development' and instead found a way of creating opportunities for participants to get some feedback and learn how to use the reflecting team model at the same time. Subsequent work with all four teams individually showed that this exercise had significantly increased energy, enthusiasm and self-belief, and enabled sufficient trust and 'optimism' to emerge to enable more complex and entrenched barriers to development to be tackled.

Further reflections

Although each team and the organization of which it is a part is unique, some common themes have emerged through our work as 'reflective consultants' in the personal social services. These are summarized below.

The fit between the demands of the work and the organizational culture Donald Schön (1983) has argued that some human service personnel cannot act as reflective practitioners in his sense, as they lack the necessary 'professional autonomy'. In our experience there is a growing tension between attempts to define practice in terms of laws and procedures (see for example DOH 1988, 1991), and the requirements of working with human beings who as well as being makers of rules are also capricious, unpredictable and creative. In itself there is nothing problematic about this tension, but it becomes a problem when its existence is denied. The boundary between practice/service delivery and management is often the point at which such tensions are played out, and the role of the front-line manager is often the key to handling this tension successfully.

Front-line managers – fish or fowl? The changing culture of personal social services organizations towards market economics is gradually shifting the identity of 'team managers', away from issues of practice and towards the management of resources (Walker 1992). However, whatever the culture of the organization, the team manager has to identify with both her 'team' and her fellow managers. Our experience is that this tension is a vital indicator of the ability of the organization to communicate effectively, especially at a time of rapid change. In most of our work with service delivery teams there has been a tendency to try and avoid exploring this tension, and the team manager often finds herself confused about what feel like conflicting loyalties. This is particularly the case in national organizations where teams are geographically isolated from their regional or national parent organization. The role of the reflective consultant is to help teams to see the potential of exploring these issues.

Gender, generation, culture and hierarchy Our work with child protection teams illustrates well the importance of exploring the fit between the work of the organization and the style of its management. Put simply, the demands of the work require extreme sensitivity to issues of generation, gender and race. At one level, these may be reflected in the organization's aims and objectives. On the other hand, the demands of the 'marketplace', legislation, and organizational procedure and precedent may require rapid adaptation and change, with maximum flexibility to re-allocate resources, or demand new skills and responses from staff. For these two aspects of organizational culture to exist in a creative tension requires great attention to the pace of change and the ability to engender trust and good communication. No amount of 'macho' style management or the commissioning of 'expert' reports from management consultants can substitute for painstaking and time-consuming consultation. In our experience time and money can be saved by approaching this with a more 'reflective' model of managing organizational change.

Managers are human too   The problem for middle managers appears to us to be that they are often ill-supported, and that their own needs for opportunities to reflect on the human dilemmas they face are subordinated to a task-centred, results-driven culture. Often, there are no formal or even informal opportunities for peer group support and sharing of feelings, with time devoted much more to the problems faced by other staff than to the pressures they experience themselves. This can make it difficult for them to appreciate the demands of service delivery staff who demand resources for their own support and consultation needs, when in some organizations middle managers are not expected to have such needs themselves. A culture can quickly develop in which status among middle managers is gained through ability not to crack under sustained pressure rather than the skills of sensitive communication and an ability to empathize with others.

Last word

'Expert' approaches to consultation seem to us to emphasize the independence, autonomy and control of the consultant, values which could be seen as representing a masculine world view. This is in contrast to valuing relationships and connections which might be associated with the feminine. In our experience, it is the relationships between these value systems and how this is played out which so often forms the focus for a reflective style of consultation. The 'resistance' which 'experts' like Sir John Harvey Jones (1990) may encounter to his proposals may be what Hoffman (1990) describes as an 'artifact' of the way the 'expert' presents himself rather than a trait of the 'mule-like' managers, or evidence of what some psychotherapists would see as 'resistance'. As reflective practitioners we aspire to the notion in the quote above from the Tao Te Ching when we receive feedback on our work. The ultimate accolade is, 'We did it!'

Acknowledgements

I would like to acknowledge the contribution of Donna Smith and Rose Hull for many of the ideas and issues raised in this chapter.

References

Andersen, T. (1987), 'The Reflecting Team: Dialogue and Meta-dialogue', *Family Process*, **26** (4) (Dec), 425–8.
Anderson, H. and Goolishian, H. (1988), 'Human Systems as Linguistic Systems:

Preliminary and Evolving Ideas about the Implications for Clinical Theory', *Family Process*, **27** (4) (Sept), 371–93.

Department of Health (1988), *Protecting Children: A Guide for Undertaking a Comprehensive Assessment*. London: HMSO.

Department of Health and the University of Bristol School of Applied Social Studies (1991), *Looking After Children: Guidelines for Users of the Assessment and Action Records*. London: HMSO.

Dimmock, B. and Dungworth, D. (1985), 'Beyond the Family: Using Network Meetings in Statutory Child Care Cases', *Journal of Family Therapy*, **7**, 45–68.

Fineman, S. (1985), *Social Work Stress and Intervention*. Aldershot: Gower.

Haley, J. (1987), *Problem Solving Therapy*, 2nd edn. San Francisco: Jossey Bass.

Harvey Jones, J. (1990), *The Trouble-shooter*. London: BBC Publications.

Hoffman, L. (1988), 'A constructivist position for family therapy', in K. Vincent (ed.), *Radical Constructivism, Autopoiesis and Psychotherapy, The Irish Journal of Psychology Special Issue*, **9** (1).

Hoffman, L. (1990), 'Constructing Realities: An Art of Lenses', *Family Process*, **29** (1) (Jan), 1–12.

Lau Tsu (sixth century BC) *Tao Te Ching* (translated by Gia-Fu Feng and Jane English 1973). London: Wildwood House.

Minuchin, S. (1974), *Families and Family Therapy*. Cambridge, MA: Harvard University Press.

Robinson, M. (1991), *Family Transformation Through Divorce and Remarriage: a Systemic Approach*. London: Routledge.

Ross, M.W. and Seeger, V. (1988), 'Determinants of Reported Burn Out in Health Professionals Associated with the Care of Patients with Aids', *Aids*, **2** (5), 295–7.

Schön, D. (1983) *The Reflective Practitioner*. New York: Basic Books.

Strong, P. and Robinson, J. (1988), *New Model Management: Griffiths and the NHS*. University of Warwick Nursing Policy Studies Centre.

Walker, A. (1992), 'Community care policy: from consensus to conflict', in J. Bornat, C. Pereira, D. Pilgrim and F. Williams (eds) *Community Care: A Reader*. Basingstoke: Macmillan.

Watzlawick, P., Weakland, J. and Fisch, R. (1974), *Change: Principles of Problem Formation and Resolution*. New York: Norton.

Yancik, R. (1984), 'Coping with Hospice Work Stress', *Journal of Psychological Oncology*, **2** (2), 19–35.

11 Finding meaning for social work in transitional times: reflections on change

Amy B. Rossiter

Two weeks ago, we took a trip to New York City. While we were there, we saw a play by Eric Bogosian called *Suburbia*. The set of the play is a convenience store parking lot, and the play concerns the lives of the young adults who hang out in the parking lot. The kids are directionless. Their various searches for meaning involve a bit of shallow political talk, based on uncompleted community college courses, drugs and alcohol, discussing their ambivalent relationship with a former friend turned rock star, and dabbling in feminist performance art. Hanging out in the parking lot is punctuated by various appearances of the Pakistani convenience store manager, who is working while putting himself through engineering school.

I felt moved and depressed by the images of the play. Here were a group of the most privileged people of the world: North American white young adults – educated, well-fed, newly emerged from child-centred parenting and pedagogy. And their lives are as barren as the parking lot they inhabit.

At the time, I attributed my feelings about the play to my concerns about my own adolescent children. Will they find a meaningful direction? Will they find passion for the world around them? It was some time after getting home from our trip that I realized that on-going ruminations about the play also came out of concern for myself. For the parking lot that is the current social space of social work and social work education at this moment in history. For my own scrabble to find meaning in social work teaching in these historical times. Consequently, this paper is a departure from previous papers I've written on social work teaching. Those papers tried to make order, to suggest routes, hint at prescriptions, to stay somehow in control of the goal. My energy at the moment is focused less on finding order in the parking lot than on finding a way to live and teach authentically as the paradigm of mainstream social work comes to a close.

The metaphor of a barren parking lot creates a bleak picture. The image is somewhat misleading as it represents only a partial fix on what Carolyn Bynum (1991) calls 'liminality' – 'a moment of suspension of normal rules and roles, a crossing of boundaries and violating of norms, that enables us to understand those norms, even (or perhaps especially) where they conflict, and move on either to incorporate or reject them' (p. 30). Liminality is also a moment of being at the threshold of the new. This in-between state of leaving the old, and not yet situated in the new characterizes social work for me at the moment. Although it is a painful and anxiety-provoking moment as social work education reforms itself, with no way of avoiding confusion, unrest and uncertainty, I also experience a sense of excitement at the possibility of examining boundaries, challenging norms and being able to articulate more urgently, aspects of social work with which I have long been at war. Thomas Kuhn (1970), in *The Structure of Scientific Revolutions*, captures this sense of possibility when he describes symptoms of transition as involving 'the proliferation of competing articulations, the willingness to try anything, the expression of explicit discontent, the recourse to philosophy and to debate over fundamentals' (p. 91).

Let me say more about why I believe we are in the midst of a liminal moment and why this has profound effects on social work education. To begin with, postmodernism has brought about a revision of epistemology that social work cannot escape. This revision means that what we have taken for granted in the past as reliable knowledge is now under dispute. This change began from several directions. It began as positivism's claim to be the sole form of legitimate knowledge began to crumble under the critique of such philosophers and social scientists as Habermas (1972), Gadamer (1992) and Fee (1986). Positivism's self-interested claim as capable of producing objective, thus 'true' knowledge fell under the revelation that there can be no such thing as knowledge that exists independent of the knower. Our background assumptions, the cultural paradigms in which our vision is shaped are active in the production of knowledge. Further, poststructuralists, particularly Michel Foucault, suggested that the production of knowledge is embedded with power: the power to produce modern subjects. From such insights, the connection between knowledge and power began to be explored. This exploration described how knowledge is inextricably linked with social control, rather than indisputably created by an independent, neutral observer. The discovery of the operation of power in knowledge has ended the fiction of the neutral gaze of the knower and ushered in the era of postpositivism.

Such a discovery has created a crisis for social work. Historically, social work allied itself with positivism in a desperate search for credibility in relation to the elite knowledges of psychiatry and psychology. Students were dutifully inducted into the notion that via statistics and method, one could know the world and one could ignore the connection between knowing and controlling. Now, it is impossible to escape postmodernism's discovery that our knowledge is deeply dependent on our social location, on the places from which we learned to see. Further, some of those locations are invested with the power to define the world in terms favourable to maintaining existing power relations. Under this condition, social work can no longer claim 'a knowledge base', but must ask instead how, by whom, and for whom social work knowledge constructs the world.

The critique of positivism coincided with the development of the new equality movements. Feminism spearheaded the space that was later opened up for race and class in order to question the relationship between knowledge and power. Feminism questioned the legitimacy of knowledge about women made in male social locations within a social context characterized by relations of domination between men and women. Thus, feminist critiques damaged the credibility of generalizations about 'human development', for example, by exposing their connections with power and domination. Social work's knowledge base has long depended on such generalizations. Maslow, Erikson and other staples of social work history simply cease to have the same uncritical status they once had.

To say this brings me a measure of relief. For some years, I have been unable to muster interest in such generalized and unitary models and schemes. It has been tortuous to teach ideas which have such little explanatory power for our times. I rejoice in the death of the possibility of studying white middle-class male college students and constructing a model of human development from the data. The shift to postmodernism, which entails the interrogation of location as it constructs knowledge and careful attention to who can speak for whom, energizes the creation of complex and useful explanations of experiences.

Concurrent with this epistemological revolution, social work education is reeling under the massive shifts in global power. In the Canadian context, one sees the erosion of the need for power to be legitimated, even through lip service, by popular will. As transnational corporations have assumed global power following over a decade of permission from neo-conservative governments, government itself has lost its role as mediator between business and labour. Given the mobility of capital, the simple threat of movement of capital ensures corporate power and diminishes any need for legitimation (Chomsky 1993). As transnationals call the shots without embarrassment, governments flounder through empty rhetoric cynically received by citizens. One of the shots that has been called is the reduction of expenditure on health, education and welfare. We are therefore trying to educate social workers in a climate where social work is ultimately controlled by the corporate agenda, with no predictable future in sight. As a method of resisting corporate power, movements for radical democracy have begun to spring up.

Morera's (1990) interpretation of Gramsci's work on radical democracy and Crosby's work on citizen panels (1986) are good examples.

It seems clear in the historical period following the demise of communism and the recognition that there is no space in the narrative of capitalism to consider human or ecological need, that a process of creating consensus about how we will meet needs will require forms of radical democracy. This thought occurs against the backdrop of the undemocratic structures of the academy and the agency. If we understand radical democracy to be connected to justice, and justice to be connected to the job of social work, how are we to deal with learning to be citizens trying to build radical democracies in existing structures? While corporate control seems to me to be tied to the image of the barren parking lot, the struggles, debates and experiments around radical democracy are at the threshold of transformation, and firmly linked to the vitality of social work.

Finally, we are now accountable for the world-shaking effects of four hundred years of theft by Western Europe and later the United States from the East and the South, theft we call colonialism. Far from simple material theft of goods, surpassing perhaps the theft of body through slavery, is the legacy of the values, beliefs, knowledges, that have allowed my white European background ancestors, and parts of my current self to live without the knowledge that we were/are thieves. These identities are identities of white privilege that are characterized by the incredible power by cultural apparatuses (Said 1978, 1993) to make others up as we need to see them: as criminals, primitives, savages clearly in need of a control that justifies exploitation. In other words, to represent others as it serves the interests of justifying theft. This is the racism which is simply part of us as social selves. And now, the colonized, through the process of decimation of nations through colonization, are moving in with the colonizer. As social workers, we bear our history and our accountability for that history in our encounters with the new service recipients: immigrants and refugees. It is within this space that the pathology-centred, psychiatry-driven models of clinical social work prove to be dismally inadequate. Categories of personal deficit have nothing to say to the waves of immigrants facing loss of homeland, resettlement, language barriers, training barriers and pervasive systemic racism.

But here too is a space for transcendence that is overwhelmingly exciting. The pressure on white racism that exists as a function of levels of immigration opens the door to ending the void and emptiness that is the underbelly of privilege. North American perspectives have been robbed of ideas about spirit through capitalism (Kovel 1991) and our ability to learn from others has been curtailed through racist ideologies that allowed us to lie about exploitation and appropriation. Here, at such a difficult time, a larger world, rich in spirit, history, difference, is a source of renewal through reflection on ourselves made possible by our exposure to the difference made accessible through migration. As social workers, we can embrace our own regeneration through valuing difference that becomes evident only after breaking out of the blinders of white racism.

I want to turn now to what impact living at this historical moment has had on me and my teaching practice. My thoughts over the past few years have been preoccupied with the meaning of the shifts of postpositivism, postmodernism, and postcolonialism for social work. In this process, most staples of social work education have simply ceased to mean anything to me. Such phrases as 'the integration of theory and practice', 'social work skills training', 'human growth and development' are for me associated with a dead paradigm. What has life and meaning for me now are unmarked paths at the threshold of the new, paths whose signposts are questions, paths that are themselves sites of uncertainty in which the only certainty I feel is my conviction that I need to be travelling on multiple but deeply interconnected paths.

One path is the vision of radical democracy as an ideal with which to resist obedience to the corporate agenda. This is a path that compels me to learn to speak when it is difficult to speak. It is a path constructed through dialogue, not prescription. It reconstitutes the nature of authority and expertise. It values facilitation and process. It eschews hierarchy. It promotes belief in human creativity. One path involves giving up on the notion that there is a fixed reality outside the knower. Instead, understanding knowing as the development and expression and dialogue between multiple perspectives developed from different locations (Haraway 1988) gives us the possibility of knowledge that understands its place in power and uses that place to replace domination with justice.

One path is what Mary Louise Pratt (1991) calls the 'contact zone'. Contact zones are the 'social spaces where cultures meet, clash, and grapple with each other, often in contexts of highly asymmetrical relations of power, such as colonialism, slavery, or their aftermaths as they are lived out in many parts of the world today'. In this contact zone, we learn how to speak to each other across divides of culture, gender and class. We know we need to speak to each other not from altruism but out of the need for self-completion, because we are missing something which is terrible to miss if whole classes of people are shut out of our consciousness because asymmetrical power makes it possible to make people up as extensions of ourselves. When we are unable to recognize difference, we lose the possibility of being recognized ourselves (Benjamin 1988).

Out of these paths, which are the only authentic places I can find in social work at the moment, can I even speak about goals for social work education? Oddly enough, it is easy enough to specify a goal, but the implications seem utterly drastic to me. I know that the goal for my classes is that we learn to recognize ourselves as people created by history who have the opportunity and responsibility to create the future. And that action towards that goal consists in having important conversations in which questions and difference are privileged over answers and similarity. But this goal is frighteningly far from 'models of social work'. It is a goal that raises questions about whether I belong. At my worst moments I am an impostor collecting money from the academy. At my best moments, I feel how much I want to oppose social work as technique, mystified theory, expert knowledge, as a privileged perspective, because I am sure that such a social work falls within discourses of domination.

Trying to live authentically in these times within the context of the social work classroom invites nothing short of perpetual anxiety for me. I have deeply internalized pedagogical forms that connote 'doing it right'. These forms ally themselves with an expert and technical social work, yet I know that letting go of such forms is crucial to my survival as a social work educator.

I would like to describe what I mean by forms. Forms are the moulds of thought and behaviour which await the input of our energy and action. The form of the classroom is a good example. At York University, Toronto, each classroom has a blackboard at the front, forty to fifty chairs with attached tables in the room, a lectern and a long table at the front of the room. It is the form for the traditional class. When students walk into the room they know their place, which is to sit in the position of the learners, and to leave the teacher's space at the front vacant for me. Lectures, teacher-prepared course outlines, examinations, answers, reproducing expert opinions, all are forms that tell us about the norms of the academy.

Educational forms, at the most subtle levels, are not physical but ideological shapes that insist on the flow of information, certainty and expertise from me to my students. In these forms, I am magically lifted out of the dilemmas of the times into a place of mastery over those dilemmas. Teaching forms somehow excuse me from wrestling with history. They enable me to talk about federal cut-backs in education and social services, but not to begin with our collective response to increased class sizes this term, or to the cuts to my grant. They make it more acceptable to talk about racism than actually to intervene in its subtle manifestations in the class itself. They draw a kind of unifying veil over the students so that I believe that students hear what I am saying in the same way, rather than each student creating what I am saying through their particularly located hearing. Mary Louise Pratt talks about the imagined classroom community that exists within teaching forms that excise students' particularity. These are forms that make us feel that we are doing it right if everybody seems to be concentrating in class and looking reasonably content and therefore producing the imaginary class community. But Pratt asks 'What is the place of unsolicited oppositional discourse, parody, resistance, critique in the imagined classroom community? Are teachers supposed to feel that their teaching has been most successful when they have eliminated such things and unified the social world, probably in their own image? Who wins when we do that? Who loses' (Pratt 1991, p. 39)? There is a way that teaching forms makes us feel successful when that imagined harmonious community is achieved. The problem is that such an achievement is at the expense of the shifts that are currently being demanded of us by the historical currents of postpositivism, postmodernism and postcolonialism.

Let me give some examples of how teaching forms, internalized as the 'right way' stand in the way of proactively articulating and reaching for a new paradigm in social work.

In one of my graduate classes, we studied the novel *Beloved* by Toni Morrison. The focus of the study was to understand how the main characters transcend their bitter inheritance of brutality through slavery. Transcendence through story-telling figures heavily in the book. At one point in the discussion, a South Asian student, 'N', burst out with great frustration 'Oh you North Americans! Catharsis, catharsis! That's all you can think about!' In that moment, she interrupted the imagined community of the classroom with the spectre of difference. Teaching forms give us many ways of bringing such moments back into line. I could have said pleasantly, 'Well, let's look at different models for change – N has a valid point here: there isn't just one model of change'. Such a comment would effectively neutralize N's difference, recreate the imagined community and render unspeakable her place at the margins of the class.

Conscious of needing to do something different, but without the forms to rely on, I looked at her weakly and said, 'Well, what do you do in India?' I felt foolish and unteacherly – not the conductor of the class symphony in which every voice joins in to create the master work, but I felt who I was – a white, North American with a very limited perspective on the rest of the world, and very abashed at my assumption of the universality of Western perspectives. N talked about concepts of fate, about meditation, about advice from elders, and about detachment, and about the capacity to tolerate contradiction. Although the class was able to use the moment to critique their own assumptions about Western universality, I was not astute enough really to capitalize on the moment. In retrospect, I realize how rich it could have been to embed N's sense of interrupting the normal and the class's insight within the reality of colonization. That view would have allowed us to look at the privileged place of catharsis in the capitalist West. We could have examined catharsis for social control aspects, for normalizing truths. We could have examined our concepts of mental health and tied them to history. In that way, through the difference introduced by the colonized living with the colonizer, as it occurred at that very moment in the class, we could have seen ourselves from another perspective and, in so doing, become more conscious of our freedom to create the future. If this had happened, I feel I could say I had done social work education in that moment. However, I have internalized teaching forms to such an extent that I didn't connect with immediate occurrence of this crucial moment in the 'contact zone', and what was ringing in my head was the course outline, the need to teach models, integrating theory and practice, and getting everybody to work harmoniously on the same goals. Somehow those goals proscribed the pain of recognizing our division into colonized and colonizer, as well as the potential joy at the possibilities that could follow our recognition of the limitations of the universalist assumptions of the West.

The next day, I was teaching an undergraduate generic practice class. I had assigned an article on refugee children. The crux of the article critiqued the lack of opportunity for children coming to Canada following traumatic experiences in their countries of origin to deal with trauma. I had thought it quite a good article, but suddenly in the middle of class, I remembered N's passionate outburst. All of the sudden, I lost the focus of the class in a haze of uncertainty. Was the article advocating catharsis, and, if so, would that represent oppression or healing to refugee children? Again, my internalized notions of teaching forms intervened, and I rather weakly referenced the issue, and I carried on as though I had some degree of mastery over the problematic. I was not able to let myself shake the need for mastery. I could not create a teachable moment by simply saying, 'I'm confused and anxious. I had an experience last night that makes me uncertain of something I previously took for granted. Can we talk about this?' Had I been able to do this, I and others would have benefited from dialogue that could have included the perspectives of the many refugees and immigrants in the class. As it was, one courageous woman talked about the experiences of her children during the refugee process, and she created an important moment for all of us, despite my confusion.

Both of these moments contained the potential to have important conversations in which we recognize our historicity and also our agency in relation to the future. Both moments can be located on the paths I described above. They both challenge the conception of knowledge as independent of the knower, and compel us to be aware of our located perspectives. They both create conditions for radical democracy when the hierarchy created by teacher certainty is destroyed by the need to learn from each other. And they both create a space for a 'contact zone', where clashes, differences and contrasts work towards reconfiguring power.

Teaching myself to spot those moments and to see them as the goal of my teaching is no easy matter. I am in the midst of planning a new course in which students' expertise, their social locations and their definitions of learning interests guide the unfolding of the course. My desire for control of the content, for predictability of the process is intense. My fantasy is that if I can achieve such predictability and controlled content, the imagined harmonious community of the classroom will naturally come about. I have to jar myself into realizing that such a community leaves us mired in a social work of false professionalization, technique, mystification, expertise and domination.

Because the pressure from internalized norms is so strong, I am keeping a quote by Hans-Georg Gadamer (1992) stapled to the front of my teaching notebook. When dominant paradigms of control and certainty threaten to encroach, I will read the following to remind myself of a hazy goal located in a not yet visible paradigm:

> The truth of experience always implies an orientation toward new experience. That is why a person who is called experienced has become so not only *through* experiences but is also open *to* new experiences. The consummation of his experience, the perfection that we call 'being experienced' does not consist in the fact that someone already knows something and knows better than any one else. Rather, the experienced person proves to be, on the contrary, someone who is radically undogmatic; who, because of the many experiences he has had and the knowledge he has drawn from them, is particularly well-equipped to have new experiences and to learn from them. The dialectic of experience has its proper fulfilment not in definitive knowledge but in the openness to new experience that is made possible by experience itself.

I am less anxious about lack of control and mastery in the classroom when Gadamer reminds me that the experienced person is radically undogmatic and open to the new, rather than a finished, closed product of theory and technique.

Another touchstone to help me change is Peggy McIntosh's (1989) work on feeling fraudulent. McIntosh describes the forces of expertise, competition, and technique as undermining personal authenticity, which she sees is the basis for legitimate authority.

> I don't think that we will be able to do what I call the meta-doubting, the necessary meta-criticism of the main invisible structures of psyche and society, until we try to get in touch with our personal senses of authenticity and talk about how things really are for us on a daily basis. Though my imagery for authenticity is personal, and therefore feels somewhat 'unintellectual' and even embarrassing, I think that we need to mine this kind of layer to reach better theoretical understanding of what our various situations are. It can help us to understand what seems wrong to us in many areas of life, including media representations of human nature, or public pronouncements and policies (p. 12).

In the final analysis, the challenge to me is to learn to take pleasure from being at a threshold. I want to be able to dive into the creative potential of this space. I believe we are in a transition from social work as an apologetic, hierarchical state function, armed with techniques garnered from theories rife with denied power to a new possibility, yet not clear, but tinged with global citizenship, with historical accountability, with self-reflexiveness and dialogue. Where the polarity between client and worker is silly. Where social work is intentional cultural work. Standing in my way are the terrors of 'not getting it right' and the fear of not belonging. I don't want to scurry back from the threshold because of these fears, but I often do.

It is unclear to me what can and should be incorporated from the old paradigm. I am all too aware that the fate of most revolutions is to reproduce old tyrannies in new forms.

I find that many concepts from mainstream clinical work are useful and helpful descriptions of people's experience. I cannot throw out the usefulness of defence mechanisms, or self-objects. But I do not know where or how to make them coherent with social work as global citizenship, and I feel that doing so is out of my reach at the moment.

Recently, two students have been trying to educate me regarding connections between spirituality and social work. They must feel terribly discouraged with the recalcitrance of their middle-aged Marxist feminist pupil. But perhaps they have been making some headway, as I catch myself thinking in terms of some kind of faith in movement, some kind of detachment . . . . Is there a space for some kind of coherence of history, politics, spirit and social work?

References

Benjamin, J. (1988), *The Bonds of Love*. New York: Pantheon.

Bynum, C. (1991), *Fragmentation and Redemption: Essays on Gender and the Human Body in Medieval Religion*. New York: Zone Books.

Chomsky, N. (1993), *The Prosperous Few and the Restless Many*. Berkeley: Odonian Press.

Crosby, N., Kelly, Janet M. and Schafer, Paul (1986), 'Citizens Panels: A New Approach to Citizen Participation', *Public Administration Review*, **46** (2), 170–78.

Fee, E. (1986), 'Critiques of modern science: the relationship of feminism to other radical epistemologies', in R. Bleier (ed.), *Feminist Approaches to Science*. New York: Pergamon Press, pp. 42–56.

Gadamer, H.–G. (1992), *Truth and Method* (Joel Weinsheimer and Donald G. Marshall, Trans.), (2nd revised edn). New York: The Crossroad Publishing Corporation.

Habermas, J. (1972), *Knowledge and Human Interests*. London: Heinemann.

Haraway, D. (1988), 'Situated Knowledges: The Science Question in Feminism and the Privilege of Partial Perspective', *Feminist Studies*, **14** (3), 575–99.

Kovel, J. (1991), *History and Spirit*. Boston: Beacon Press.

Kuhn, T. (1970), *The Structure of Scientific Revolutions*. Chicago: University of Chicago Press.

McIntosh, P. (1989), *Feeling Like a Fraud: Part Two*, Working Paper Series No. 37. The Stone Center for Developmental Services and Studies.

Morera, E. (1990), 'Gramsci and Democracy', *Canadian Journal of Political Science/ Revue Canadienne de Science Politique,* **23** (1), 23–37.

Pratt, M.L. (1991), 'Arts of the Contact Zone', *Profession,* **91**, 33–40.

Said, E. (1978), *Orientalism.* New York: Vintage.

Said, E. (1993), *Culture and Imperialism.* New York: Alfred A. Knopf.

12 Reflective learning, social work education and practice in the 21st century

Imogen Taylor

As we approach the 21st century, social work educators and practitioners are faced with the imperative of responding to far-reaching changes. The prospects for social work education and practice may either be viewed as bleak and daunting, or alternatively as exciting and challenging. In this chapter, I begin by identifying some of the key themes which have emerged from the different contributions about reflective learning included in this book. I then highlight some of the fundamental changes facing society, social work education and practice today, and suggest that reflective learning is one approach which can equip students to respond to the rapidly changing world they will be practising in.

Key themes

Eight themes are highlighted here because they recur throughout this book. This is neither an inclusive list of key issues associated with reflective learning, nor a summary of what different contributors say. To impose a unifying framework would be inappropriate and restrict the creativity and innovation which reflective learning is designed to generate. Yet, the recurrence of these themes suggests they may be central to reflective learning and potentially to social work education in the future.

The first theme identified is that it is not enough to teach students knowledge for practice, students must learn how to use knowledge in practice. Students must acquire the ability to reflect on how they think and act in practice, and what the implications are. As they encounter new and unpredictable situations, social workers must be able to make critically reflexive judgements and decisions, and know how to transfer appropriate knowledge and skills from situations already encountered. The competence

153

approach suggests theory can be neatly and systematically applied to practice, yet inevitably theory must be mediated by the social worker to be useful and applicable. As Catherine Papell (Chapter 2) clearly states, an essential part of the process of mediation is for the student to be aware of his/her subjectivity and know the emotional world of self. There are a number of interesting examples of authors reflecting on their own subjectivities.

The capacity to reflect in response to new situations without reacting with immediate answers to questions which almost certainly are not fully formulated, requires being able to contain anxiety generated by confusion, uncertainty and unpredictability. Reflective learning is by its nature not prescriptive and inevitably does not follow an ordered sequential pattern. Not only is this a challenge for the student or practitioner, but also for the educator and practice teacher, manager and team leader, who have to contain their own anxiety and that of others. The experience of seeing students emerge from such uncertainty with an increased sense of self-agency validates the approach, 'they come to see themselves as actors who can influence relationships even in the most constraining of social work bureaucracies' (Moffatt, Chapter 5, page 59).

The discussion in this book suggests reflective learning generates creative as opposed to programmed responses. There is a variety of rich descriptions of innovative approaches to learning in the classroom and practice. Interestingly, reflective approaches to management and team work have also generated innovation and creativity (Chapters 9 and 10). Several authors refer to how the style and nature of relationships between people at one level in an organization will influence relationships at other levels. The process of teaching reflective practice both mirrors and models the process of reflective practice with service users, and may in turn be enacted in team management and the management of the wider organization. There is undoubtedly a tension between reflective learning which stimulates creativity and the external requirements of professional accrediting bodies and institutions of higher education. Such tension is most acutely felt in assessment processes, however, it is suggested that learning to manage such tension is part of the process of learning to practice.

The importance in reflective learning of a dialogue between the educator and learner, team leader and team member, manager and staff is referred to by a number of authors. This notion of interconnectedness which is also found in femininist theory, challenges traditional concepts of power in education, particularly the concept of the expert–novice hierarchy (Taylor 1996 forthcoming). Clearly, the educator in professional education must hold power as the gatekeeper to the profession, but if such power is openly identified and managed this enables acknowledgement of the power of the student consumer and encourages a real dialogue to take place.

For reflective learning to occur there must be a coherent framework of learning structures which enable students to engage in activities which promote reflective learning, including reflective learning in field placements (Chapters 4 and 8). Authors describe a variety of activities including learning journals, role plays, videos and the use of art materials. Such a framework must also incorporate decisions made about the place of formal knowledge and must support critical thinking and systematic analysis. Nick Gould suggests (Chapter 6) that there is a risk of a 'quagmire of relativism' in adopting a constructivist view of knowledge and whereas in a 'pure' liberal progressive model of education this might be acceptable, in professional education inevitably standards must be met. The challenge is to establish activities which promote reflective learning within a framework of course requirements.

David Boud and Susan Knights suggest we need to develop a discourse for discussing reflection in learning (Chapter 3) and contributions from international authors have made us very conscious of the challenge of terminology. Certainly there are some contradictions embedded in, for example, framing reflective learning as a 'dialogue' between 'teacher' and 'student'. Similarly the language of 'management' is unsatisfactory, although we continue to use it in the absence of a sufficiently established alternative. Existing terms are beginning to be used in new ways and terms new to social work education, such as 'facilitator' (Chapter 7), are being introduced. Inevitably there is an initial self-consciousness in using such terms, but with time they acquire a common currency.

Several authors refer to the power of metaphor and imagery in reflective learning. Amy Rossiter's metaphor (Chapter 11) of standing at a threshold appears aptly to represent the experience of social work educators today as we look to the future. We want to be able to see the creative potential of what lies ahead and not turn away or impose premature closure because of our fears. The metaphor of a threshold raises the question of what to take with us from the old paradigms. Amy Rossiter identifies the paradigms she would be reluctant to leave behind but other educators writing in this book, were they asked the same question, may select different items of importance to carry over the threshold.

Finally, a theme which recurs throughout this book is that of difference and diversity. Whereas some commonality and uniformity is inevitable and essential because of the ultimate shared destination of qualified social work and the need for common standards, reflective learning allows for and supports diversity, crucial to managing the transition into the next century. Linked with the theme of integrating difference and diversity with common standards is the issue of assessment as it relates to reflective learning. This is an area where we are aware of an urgent need for further developmental work. One of the most significant challenges for educators is to develop assessment tools which enhance reflective learning at the same time as they support the requirement for common standards, to develop, for example, mechanisms for self- and peer-assessment, crucial for self-appraisal and life-long learning, and link these to existing conventional assessment tools.

Postmodernity, social work and social work education

As we stand at the threshold, one certainty is that we are facing an unpredictable situation in relation to the future of both social work practice and education. In postmodern society, the direction to take is far from clear, the map appears to offer the certainty of short-cuts, such as a focus on competence, yet there are warning signs that following such a path will lead to a narrow one-way street with social workers as bureaucratic gatekeepers to the resources which lie beyond.

A cogent critique of postmodernity and social work is offered by Nigel Parton in two complementary articles where he discusses the nature and possible futures for contemporary social work in a period of considerable change and uncertainty (Parton 1994a, 1994b). Parton defines modernity as a term which refers to the cluster of economic, political and social systems which became increasingly pervasive in the nineteenth and twentieth centuries. A central feature of modernity is the recognition that 'human order is neither natural nor God-driven but essentially vulnerable and contingent but can, by the development and application of science, be subject to human control' (1994a, p. 27). However, as Parton documents (1994a), the twentieth century has seen profound changes occurring at all levels in developed societies which have undermined this vision of order associated with modernity. Postmodernity 'is characterised by a fragmentation of modernity into forms of institutional pluralism, marked by variety, contingency, relativism and ambivalence' (1994, p. 28). At its bleakest are the kinds of images described by Amy Rossiter (Chapter 11) as she reflects on the meaning of the play set in the parking lot of a New York convenience store.

In postmodern society, social work is experienced as particularly vulnerable to tensions, ambiguity and fragmentation. Parton suggests that in modern society casework provided a unifying force with its emphasis on a systematic approach to practice, its coherent knowledge base derived from psychodynamic theory, and its bringing together from a variety of agencies social workers carrying diverse roles and responsibilities. However, in postmodern society social work does not have a core, or an underlying knowledge base and legitimacy, 'there is a hole in the centre of the enterprise' (p. 101). In the absence of such unity, notions of planning and management become more central. As Nick Gould discusses (Chapter 1), employers and

yts
1.F.

. V. - Operational
gym - Operational

— S/lifts
anteen

gym - operational
1' floor - operational

Fem hearing soap √ roll √ gl rail √ h/dryer presentable

1 M FEW/ Soap √ roll √ h/dryer √ gl rail X

gym - soap √ roll √ gl rail - present X h/d facilities

. LO soap X roll √ h/dryer √ gl rail √ satisfactory

LO vent off roll X soap X gl rail √ hand/dryer √ - presentable

. LO - soap √ roll √ gl rail √ h/dryer - presentable

PRESENTATION OF THE GCSE LAW COURSEWORK

On the front page of each piece of work to be submitted, candidates should give the following information, with the assignment commencing on the second page:

(a) the candidate's name and examination number;

(b) **the centre's name and number;** 7144 7...

(c) the component code (3161/C);

(d) the examination session; *Summer 03'*

(e) the title of the piece of work;

(f) a list of sources on which the answer is based.

THE COURSEWORK MAY BE HANDWRITTEN, TYPED OR WORD-PROCESSED.

the new managerialism are allied in the drive to manage uncertainty, pushing inexorably towards certainty with the development of a new discourse of management which upholds monitoring, evaluation and assessment as central mechanisms of control.

Higher education is also subject to an increasingly complex pattern of pressures of demand and supply, and is no longer 'a secret garden' (Barnett 1992, p. 8). To help analyse these influences and their implications for student learning, Jarvis (1993) proposes four models of education: the welfare model where education puts right structural injustice; the market model where education is a commodity and the emphasis is on competition and efficiency; the social control model where education has become part of the agenda of the New Right and is shaped by the demands of employers; and, the progressive liberalism model where education enriches the individual.

The moves to increase access of those students traditionally disadvantaged in gaining entry to higher education reflect an acknowledgement of the welfare model of education (Taylor 1996 forthcoming). However, in the United Kingdom, analysis of access data reveals a disturbing picture of lack of change, 'class, gender and ethnicity are now the three giants in the path of aspirations towards equity, replacing what was the major focus of traditional concern with social class' (Halsey 1993, p. 129). Change in relation to gender is the most encouraging, but in the United Kingdom we lag far behind developments in Australia and Canada (Blackburn and Jarman 1993). Access patterns for ethnic minority applicants are variable depending on which ethnic minority the applicant represents, and whether the applicant is seeking entry to 'old' or 'new' universities. For example, only half as many Afro-Caribbean as white applicants are likely to succeed in gaining admission to old universities (Modood 1993). Finally, the giant sleeping the longest and the most impervious to change is that of social class (Egerton and Halsey 1993). However, data is generally not available to provide a clear picture of what happens once students from disadvantaged groups gain access to higher education, and how accessible they find the courses they embark on, with the result that we do not yet know whether education is effectively putting right a structural injustice.

Under the influence of the New Right and Conservative rhetoric, the market and social control models appear to be merging in mutual interest. These links are addressed by Watson (1992) who suggests that there are three interest groups, sponsors who include the professions, government and employing agencies; providers who include higher education institutions; and clients who include students. There are indications that the number of interest groups is proliferating and alliances are changing with the result that control of both higher education and the professions is increasingly in the hands of government and employers.

First, the sponsor group of professions, government and employing agencies appear to form an uneasy triangular relationship of shifting alliances with government and employers tending to cohere in an attempt to control the profession. This pattern is not particular to social work and is also evident in other professions such as teaching, and to a lesser extent health care professions and the law. Government led initiatives such as NCVQ (National Council for Vocational Qualifications) and EHE (Enterprise in Higher Education) emphasize operationalism and instrumental learning and increase employer involvement at the cost of professional control. This is reflected particularly in the development of the competence approach which, if narrowly interpreted, trains social workers to practise in more regulated and regulating ways (Cannan 1994–1995).

Secondly, the provider groups of higher and professional education have traditionally been uneasy allies, with higher education giving priority to propositional knowledge, and professional education giving priority to personal and process knowledge (Eraut 1992). At a time when it would make strategic sense for these two sub-groups to come together, they may be further diverging. For example, the increasing pre-eminence of the HEFCE Research Assessment Exercise in determining funding enhances the priority given to propositional knowledge, whereas developments in social work education and practice are pushing social work towards an alliance with employers, with increasingly scarce time and resources devoted to structures such as partnerships with agencies.

Finally, in relation to the client interest group, there is some evidence that the marketization of higher education, given a recent push in the UK by the transformation of polytechnics to 'new' universities, increases the power of the student consumer (Cannan 1994–1995). 'Service users, (passengers, students, patients, clients) become customers in the project of marketisation' (Cannan, p. 7). In addition, in social work there is a newly emerging interest group of service users given impetus by the philosophy of user-led practice enshrined in recent legislation such as the Children Act (1989) and the National Health Service and Community Care Act (1990). Service users are beginning to play a role in social work education (Beresford and Croft 1990; Beresford and Harding 1993) which is potentially highly significant and may be one of the most exciting challenges ahead for educators. One outcome of this development is that user involvement, like student involvement, increases unpredictability in the classroom and challenges the power and control of the educator. At this stage it is unclear whether service users and student consumers will form an alliance. There is a strong argument for users being identified as another group of providers of higher education, and certainly when users are organized in groups, such as psychiatric survivors or disabled people, their provider role in student learning is potentially influential.

The progressive liberalism model designed to enrich the individual is still to be found in pockets in higher education, and at first sight seems the most likely home for reflective learning. However, progressive liberalism has taken a battering from the alliance of market and social control models, particularly given the pervasive influence of operationalism or instrumental learning (Barnett 1993), which encourages reproductive rather than deep learning (Marton et al 1984), and restricts individual choice. A split between the progressive liberalism model and social work education appears accentuated by the trend in recent years for outcomes required of qualifying social workers to be conceptualized as competences. However, in the final section of this chapter I will argue that competence-based learning and reflective learning are not mutually incompatible and may indeed complement each other and have mutual roles to play in the market model of education.

Reflective learning and postmodernism

Reflective learning may be conceptualized as a response to postmodernism, as a positive and creative approach to the prospect of living with contingency. The competence approach may also be perceived as a response to postmodernism and the result of a quest for certainty. It is suggested that reflective learning and competence have the potential to be more compatible than is initially apparent. If the competence approach is broadly conceptualized, reflective learning offers the opportunity of providing a crucial component. Whereas, if narrowly defined, the competence approach is reductionist and focuses on discrete observable behaviours, denying the importance of the process of learning, the need to integrate skills or apply knowledge, or the importance of creativity and innovation (Cannan 1994–1995).

Gonczi (1994), in his analysis of competence as it relates to the professions of teaching and law in Australia, advocates an integrated approach to competence where a complex combination of attributes (knowledge, values and skills) are used to understand and function within the particular situation in which professionals find themselves. Underlying attributes such as critical thinking and the need for reflective practice are identified as essential to professional practice. This approach to competence acknowledges the shift to viewing knowledge as product, yet at the same time retains a crucial emphasis on knowledge as process (Scott 1984), thus integrating competence and reflective learning.

It is also suggested that reflective practice can play an essential part in the market model of social work education and practice. In a world of uncertainty and rapid change, reflective learning offers the potential for learning how to learn and how to practise in a self-determined way in situations where the unknown and unpredictable are being faced. Reflective learning fits with the market requirement for self-appraisal and lifelong learning. For practice in postmodern society, students must develop the capacity not so much to know, as to be able to deploy learning capacities to enable them to operate effectively (Barnett 1993, p. 35). The development of internally referential systems is crucial, 'where nothing can be taken for granted and where there are no self-evident truths available or waiting to be found the reflexive, self-monitoring, individual becomes crucial to making sense of the world and trying to impose a degree of consistency and control upon it' (Parton 1994b, p. 106). As our contributors have identified, it is equally crucial for institutions to develop reflexivity, for unless reflexivity operates at all levels of education and practice, it is unlikely to survive.

References

Barnett, R. (1993), 'Knowledge, Higher Education, and Society: A Postmodern Problem', *Oxford Review of Education*, **19** (1), 33–46.

Barnett, Ronald (1992), 'What effects? What outcomes?', in Ronald Barnett (ed.), *Learning to Effect*. Buckingham: SRHE and Open University Press.

Blackburn, R. and Jarman, J. (1993), 'Changing Inequalities in Access to British Universities', *Oxford Review of Education*, **19** (2), 197–215.

Beresford, P. and Croft, S. (1990), 'A Sea Change', *Community Care*, 4 October.

Beresford, P. and Harding, T. (eds) (1993), *A Challenge to Change. Practical Experiences of Building User-Led Services*. London: National Institute for Social Work.

Cannan, C. (1994–1995), 'Enterprise Culture, Professional Socialisation, and Social Work Education in Britain', *Critical Social Policy*, **2**, 5–18.

Egerton, M. and Halsey, A.H. (1993), 'Trends by Social Class and Gender in Access to Higher Education', *Oxford Review of Education*, **19** (2), 183–95.

Eraut, M. (1992), 'Developing the knowledge base: a process perspective on professional education', in R. Barnett (ed.), *Learning to Effect*. Buckingham: SRHE and Open University Press.

Gonczi, A. (1994), 'Competency Based Assessment in the Professions in Australia', *Assessment in Education*, **1** (1), 27–44.

Halsey, A.H. (1993), 'Trends in Access and Equity in Higher Education: Britain in International Perspective', *Oxford Review of Education*, **19** (2), 129–40.

Jarvis, P. (1993), *Adult Education and the State: Towards a Politics of Adult Education*. London: Routledge.

Marton, F. et al (eds) (1984), *The Experience of Learning*. Edinburgh: Scottish Academy Press.

Modood, T. (1993), 'The Number of Ethnic Minority Students in British Higher Education: Some Grounds for Optimism', *Oxford Review of Education*, **19** (2), 167–82.

Parton, N. (1994a), 'Problematics of Government, (Post) Modernity and Social Work', *British Journal of Social Work*, **24** (1), 9–32.

Parton, N. (1994b), 'The Nature of Social Work under Conditions of (Post) Modernity', *Social Work and Social Sciences Review*, **5** (2), 93–112.

Scott, P. (1984), *The Crisis of the University*. Beckenham: Croom Helm.

Taylor, I. (forthcoming), *Developing Learning in Professional Education*. Milton Keynes: Open University Press.

Taylor, I. (1996, forthcoming), 'Enquiry and Action Learning: empowerment in social work education', in S. Jackson and M. Preston-Shoot (eds), *Educating Social Workers in a Changing Policy Context*. London: Whiting and Birch.

Watson, D. (1992), 'The changing shape of professional education', in H. Bines and D. Watson, *Developing Professional Education*. Buckingham: SRHE and Open University Press.

Index